Protecting Clients from Fraud, Incompetence, and Scams

LANCE WALLACH

WILEY

John Wiley & Sons, Inc.

Published by John Wiley & Sons, Inc., Hoboken, New Jersey.
Published simultaneously in Canada.

For general information on our other products and services or for technical
support, please contact our Customer Care Department within the United States
at (800) 762-2974, outside the United States at (317) 572-3993 or fax (317)
572-4002.

Wiley also publishes its books in a variety of electronic formats. Some content
that appears in print may not be available in electronic books. For more
information about Wiley products, visit our web site at www.wiley.com.

Library of Congress Cataloging-in-Publication Data:

Wallach, Lance.
  Protecting clients from fraud, incompetence, and scams / Lance Wallach.
    p. cm.
  Includes index.
  ISBN 978-0-470-53974-3 (cloth)
  1. Fraud–Prevention. I. Title.
  HV6691.W35 2010
  362.88–dc22

                                                                2009037068

Printed in the United States of America

10 9 8 7 6 5 4 3 2 1

Contents

Acknowledgments

I wish to express my sincere thanks to everyone who contributed to the creation of this book. An "instructional" tome of this nature, by design, relies, from the moment of inception to the last run off the presses, on the advice and input of highly qualified experts. Although many have contributed their expertise in various forms and fashions, I would be remiss if I did not single out and acknowledge the contributions of some people in particular.

Mark Boehm, MBA, CWPP™, was instrumental in pulling this book together. His contributions in terms of content were outstanding, and his editorial commentary improved the flow and delivery of information tremendously. His expertise was invaluable.

Mr. Boehm received his Bachelor of Science (BS) degree from Cornell University School of Agriculture and Life Sciences, and Master of Business Administration (MBA) degree from Southern Methodist University. He is a principal with Alpha Wealth Management, a boutique financial services firm providing asset protection, tax reduction, and advanced financial planning strategies for high-net-worth clientele. Mr. Boehm serves as an expert consultant on all things life insurance related—planning techniques, life settlements (retail and institutional), and captive insurance.

Thank you, Mark, for all your help and input.

Carl Allen III's input regarding forensic accounting investigation was key. Carl is the owner of Allen Financial Services,

LLC. He is a graduate of North Carolina State University (BS Mathematics, 1972) and Durham Technical Community College (AAS Accounting, 1976). Mr. Allen is currently a member of the Association of Certified Fraud Examiners, the National Association of Tax Professionals, and the National Society of Tax Professionals. He is a volunteer representative for the NC State University Student Aid Association, and provides support and resources for Elon University students pursuing opportunities through their career center.

Mr. Allen has served in various financial management positions over the past 30 years with companies in the insurance and construction industries. He provides accounting and technical support for small businesses in the areas of: fraud investigations, interim accounting management support, accounting and project consulting, and income tax preparation and planning.

Thanks, Carl.

Aaron Skloff, AIF, CFA, MBA, provided much of the content for this book. Let me outline for you briefly a few of his accomplishments so you can understand the level of advice you're about to receive.

Mr. Skloff received a Bachelor of Science (BS) degree in accounting from Pennsylvania State University's Smeal College of Business and Master of Business Administration (MBA) degree in finance from New York University's Stern School of Business. He is a Chartered Financial Analyst (CFA), a member of the CFA Institute (formerly the Association for Investment Management and Research) and an Accredited Investment Fiduciary (AIF).

He has taught finance courses through Rutgers University. His equity research reports have been published on the two largest financial research databases, First Call and Multex. During the course of his professional career, he has been cited by the *Associated Press, BusinessWeek, Dow Jones, Fortune,*

Princeton Business Journal, Reuters, Wall Street Journal, and other news organizations.

Mr. Skloff is CEO of Skloff Financial Group, a register investment advisor firm based in Berkeley Heights, New Jersey. The firm specializes in financial planning, investment management, and risk management for individuals and families and group benefit for employers.

Thank you, Aaron.

I'd also like to gratefully extend my sincere appreciation to all the people from John Wiley & Sons who were instrumental in bringing this book to press.

Lance Wallach

Introduction

Every Accountant and Attorney Should Read This Book

Honey, I forgot to duck...
—World Heavyweight Champion Jack Dempsey after losing
the heavyweight title to Gene Tunney in 1926

For better or worse, it is the year of Bernie Madoff. His investment firm, a hollow Trojan Horse parked on Wall Street, was emblematic of a financial system that strangled itself on opportunistic lies about complexity and global markets.

Complexity in volatile trading markets certainly exists, but too often the fund packaging nomenclature was used to shield mediocre and abysmally poor fund managers from the results of their shenanigans, operating as a buffer between the managers and their clients. Arias for what used to be called merely "trading" became surgery on financial instruments and rebundled new packages.

The problem, as one analyst said, was that these people claimed sophistication but they had no artistry.

In the arts and finance, people follow stars.

Once Bernard L. Madoff's mysterious but outperforming methodology gained public traction, the volume of investors lined up to suck on the teat of putative success and was the line around the block in posh zip codes. Business owner–investors might have camped out in line, too, but they needed to be at work in the morning to face the constant purveyors of erosion to their businesses.

Madoff Investment Securities garnered much privately held largesse. And yet, believe it or not, there may be worse players out there than "the Bernster." Corporate workers know their 401(k)s or pension incentive plans are faring to the bad side lately.

If workers want to feel better, they should look west—to California to be exact. The Sunshine State holds publicly funded asset pension trusts as large as a roundup of third-world debtor nations. Guess how much they've lost recently? If you're a public employee, you need to know, and you need to know why. If you're a business owner, you also need to know how and why.

The key margin is the players between corporate and public entities. That would be you—small- and mid-size business owner–investors. As if you're not burdened enough, no longer can you afford to let a rising stock market raise all boats—drownings, sharks, and icebergs have already been sighted.

You cannot afford to calculate mystery black box schemes perpetrated by former NASDQ Chairs—one Bernard Madoff to be exact. Due diligence in all phases of business operations seems in order. This diligence will require no sleep for the next, oh, 10 to 20 years.

Not really, if you can answer one basic question:

Why don't "experts" read the IRS code like a medical school manual of surgery?

Answer(s):

First, there aren't that many "experts," and those that are seek to keep a low profile (in comparison to TV talking heads who make their money from boob tube salaries, not real-world contingencies), because they have had a loyal clientele for decades. The sad news is—they don't need you; in fact, they probably couldn't fit you into their mad schedule.

Second, capitalism does share in archetypes that fly below the radar (because they're legal strategies) and rewards due diligence with annual gains rather than one-time overlarge payouts (the latter used to be called gambling).

Third, a team approach to business investing, utilizing a tax strategist, insurance—legal specialist and financial planner, who actually talk to and meet one another—will, in the long run, outperform the one-shot wonders.

In this book, we provide you the blueprint. You need to take the necessary actions. Business owner–investors are the middle layer between public service–government organizations and multinational corporations. You are the serious music the U.S. dream and economy thrive upon.

I would say you need to learn how to box.

CHAPTER 1

Meltdown

Muhammad Ali: Superman don't need no seat belt.
Flight Attendant: Superman don't need no plane, neither.

The U.S. financial system meltdown has grimly scythed decades of accumulated business profit, investment, and personal wealth. As we have seen, investors undervalued their own rationality and overvalued chaotic wealth management schemes masquerading as complex asset management in a global economy. Investors dumped business earnings, pension assets, and personal funds into investment portfolios without due diligence as to the logic and structural soundness of those investments and their strategic economic orientation.

Counterintuitively, many wealthy investors and business owners took leaps of faith with hard-won assets into complex investment schemes they didn't understand because returns were bountiful. The hard work processes by which investors grew their businesses or their wealth did not seem to apply to strategically marketed programs devised by Wall Street wizards. "The wizards must be smarter and more inventive" was the mantra. It was an era where not paying attention yielded robust earnings.

1

The Party's Over

The charlatans have now been revealed and returning to earth awash in lost assets has been a hard lesson learned for many business and personal investors. Fear of any kind of strategy beyond the most basic principles of accounting math has turned financial markets into rigid, ossified institutions. Credit is tight; doubt is rampant. But fear need not overtake common sense. If one is strategically poised to act, there are methods to reap opportunities even within the constant inhalation of a bad news economy.

There are ways to maximize wealth assets through sound tax strategies aimed at reducing exposure to IRS audits, while freeing liquidity for further investment income growth. Part of the picture is understanding what the U.S. government has and has not done in the financial sector.

The U.S. government failed to regulate its own legislative loosening of the credit and investment markets. The government allowed financial businesses that previously dealt in single issue items, such as credit allocation (banks), insurance (insurance companies), and tax protection (accounting firms) to become full-service investment/banking/insurance hundred-headed hydras. With the ability to manipulate different asset classes, many of these businesses grew astronomically by forging new markets out of fringe niches and clients they previously would not have pursued.

Much of the growth was built on Ponzi-type schemes of trading one asset class for another, rebundling (while claiming it was an asset protection maneuver), and charging transaction and management fees for transferring and translating assets into different holding tanks. Ethical portfolio diversity became a joke.

Forensic auditors will spend years trying to unravel the origination of lost portfolios and their mutation into worthless products that propped up marketing schemes.

2

We All Know the Result

Because the government was involved in allowing multipurpose financial institutions to pursue growth by any means necessary, the government now stands confused, dazed, and unable to act under the fallout from the variety and volume of reckless financial transactions it helped perpetuate. In fact, it is throwing more money into the hollow house called Wall Street, assuming that the perpetrators will suddenly ethically encumber themselves and fix the problem.

Meanwhile, the Security and Exchange Commission (SEC), the so-called regulatory agency of the U.S. financial system, is like a lost orphan, its budget miniscule in comparison to the largesse tossed to the big dog bankers and their pals. Shouldn't the budget allocation be the opposite until we have reviewed and identified the malfeasance that brought down the system?

There is another looming storm on the horizon that could swamp any economic lifeboats sent out into the water by the government. There is the potential for a catastrophic failure of retirement funds in the United States, affecting nearly one-third of the pension plans existent. With baby boomers set to retire in massive numbers, such a failure would further erode a weak, destabilized economy.

In 2006 Congress passed the Pension Protection Act, mandating that companies with defined benefit pension programs be fully funded, as measured by the ability to pay out money to all retirees should the latter decide to withdraw their accrued assets. Of the 500 largest U.S. companies, more than 200 do not meet the Pension Protection Act standard in 2009.

Standard & Poor's 1500 Index of corporations reveals how dire the situation has become: The Index corporations moved from a $60 billion pension plan surplus at the end of 2007 to $409 billion deficit before the end of 2008. Defined benefit pensions (usually, where an employee payroll deduction is matched by the company into the employee's retirement fund) at these companies are part of a potential nightmare scenario even in good economic times, and we are entering an undefined period of economic uncertainty and groping in the dark.

When revenues decline in an economic crunch, payroll must be met at salaries that haven't declined. In the worst situation, a company may have to decide between meeting payroll and matching payroll-defined pension requirements. Corporate pension funds are troubled and clearly face the problem of underfunding. Many of the corporate pension funds invest their money conservatively. There are, however, a group of pension fund managers who have not invested conservatively or wisely and they are the first wave of a larger pension fund tsunami that could catapult the U.S. economy into a stunning freefall.

The snowball rolls downhill: jobs are cut, stocks consistently trend downward, reducing a company's investment stream, destabilizing the stock market and the company's ability to remain productive or even solvent.

Public pension funds and federal retirement accounts hold approximately $3.5 trillion in their accounts. There is another $1 trillion in unionized corporate workers who are part of the management team deciding fund investments. Together, these funded retirement vehicles cover approximately 27 million Americans and account for more than 30 percent of the U.S. retirement pension fund system. A failure of 30 percent of the system would be catastrophic to United States and international markets and to the personal retirement benefits of the invested potential pensioners.

Grim Statistics

The bad news is that 30 percent was at risk before the current financial meltdown. The worse news is some pensions are close to defaulting without cash infusions that would have to come from taxpayers, necessitating higher taxes, less spending, and an unprecedented economic crisis stretching into the foreseeable future. Consider these numbers:

By 2008, just before the stock market began to tank, an estimated 40 percent of union-led pension funds were undercapitalized, meaning there was no guarantee the funds had enough money on hand to pay out member benefits.

California has two of the largest pension funds in the country: CalPERS, which is the biggest U.S. pension fund, covers California public employees, and CalSTRS, the state teacher pension fund. Their combined assets, at their zenith in 2007, weighed in at more than $400 billion, more than the GDP of some nations. By February 2009, the funds had lost 26 percent of their value from July 2008. CalPERS was more than 100 percent funded in summer 2007; it is currently at 70 percent (funding) and declining.

Adding to an already grim picture is CalPERS unaccounted investment in the California real estate market, which has descended faster than most markets nationwide. Things are not looking much better for 2009. In February, LandSource Communities Development, which owns 15,000 acres north of Los Angeles, announced it was filing for bankruptcy protection. The property developer's backer? None other than CalPERS.

The California city of Vallejo filed for bankruptcy in May 2008, in great measure because of an insolvent public pension fund. San Diego's pension fund deficit may cause it to follow Vallejo into the abyss.

Connecticut's state pension fund is estimated to be only 50 percent funded in comparison to its membership base.

Underfunded VEBAs (Voluntary Employee Beneficiary Associations) have been used by corporations to negotiate their way out of seemingly intractable health cost-pension plan obligations. The Big Three automakers recently negotiated VEBA agreements with their union employees, transferring $56.5

billion to a United Auto Workers (UAW)–managed retiree health care VEBA, allowing the parent corporation to erase $88.7 billion in long-term pension obligations.

The math says there is an immediate $30 billion-plus funding shortage. Union VEBA management will be crucial; there is no corporate safety net should the plan fail. UAW president Ron Gettelfinger said the General Motors VEBA would be safe for 80 years, but the recent track record for underfunded VEBAs is not good.

For instance:

Caterpillar transferred $32.3 million to a UAW retiree health plan in 1998. The fund was bankrupt by 2004. Renegotiation and lawsuits ensued. Also in 2004, a UAW-Detroit Diesel health care fund was depleted, resulting in more legal action.

The GM VEBA will probably fail. If UAW projections are wrong, for example, about the rate of increase in health care costs, they will be woefully wrong about how long this fund will remain solvent. The cost of health care escalates each year and the money used to seed the VEBA was not enough to begin with. Health care increases were estimated by the UAW at 5 percent, with invested VEBA funds increasing by 9 percent. The scenario could turn out to be exactly the opposite, or worse.

Prior to 2008's meltdown, comparative studies between public and private employee investment programs indicated a burgeoning problem in the former. A study of 200 state and local pension funds from 1968 to 1986, performed and analyzed by Olivia Mitchell, executive director of the Pension Research Council at the Wharton School, discovered that public pension investments substantially underperformed against other pooled funds, and quite frequently below market indexes.

The evisceration of public pension funds began before recent economic quagmires. Prior to the 1970s the funds were managed conservatively, utilizing fiduciary methods aimed at protecting the future pensioners and tax payers, who end up footing the bill if a fund defaults.

Three things changed in the 1970s and into the 1980s:

1. Politicians began to get involved in the direction of fund management.
2. Pension fund managers began to "play" emerging markets and potential sources of elevated revenue: corporate bonds, stocks, foreign instruments, real estate, private equity companies, and hedge funds.
3. Union and public employee pension funds initiated, sometimes against membership understanding or wishes, a transfer of assets into socially responsible investments. Investment research company Morningstar said that as of November 2008, 76 of 91 socially responsible stock funds were performing at sub-Dow levels. Last December, the Sierra Club's social fund liquidated its assets due to consistent losses.

All three of these developments have accumulated negatively; the union and public pension fund system is in total woefully underfunded. The default costs, combined with recession, deflation, and the stimulus plans guaranteed to raise taxes, would be difficult to recoup except by further tax increases, promoting the vicious depressive economic environment in which we are currently embroiled.

If public pension funds cannot meet their obligations to cover promised member benefits, the only available resource to siphon money from will be taxpayers—the same taxpayers who are watching their personal retirement portfolios fall off a cliff. As a business owner, you need to protect yourself and your assets with a smart tax and investment strategy.

It is crucial that the small business owner understand tax and investment strategies that not predicated on traditional pension planning methods. Business survival may be at stake.

Care must be taken, though, in assessing and choosing the right option.

Retirement Plans and the IRS

A VEBA, 412(e)(3) plan or a 401(k) plan may be the proper fit for your business and investment strategy, but the IRS will be watching carefully how you form and operate your plan. We discuss the pluses and minuses of these plans further on in the book. A cash-hungry IRS can scrutinize the legitimacy of any of these pension planning methods. It is essential to use the tools, advice, and strategy of competent tax and investment strategists.

The odds are stacked against the average investor, it seems. The opposite is true, however—if the average investor is willing to educate himself and team up with ethical professionals who have weathered this storm, and will weather the next one, too.

One thing is certain, though; when the government is teetering toward insolvency it will seek to make up lost revenues. Over the next 12 months, the Small Business and Self-Employed Division (SB/SE) of the Internal Revenue Service will focus on taxpayer services and increased enforcement. SB/SE owns the majority of the tax gap. Enforcement is a necessary presence when you are talking about tax administration. Let us review a cautionary tale regarding the methods it can utilize.

Bruce Hink, who has given me permission to utilize his name and circumstances, is a perfect example of what the IRS is doing to unsuspecting business owners. What follows is a story about Bruce Hink and how the IRS fined him $200,000 a year for being in what they called "a listed transaction." In addition, I believe that the accountant who signed the tax return and the insurance agent who sold the retirement plan will each be fined $200,000 as material advisors. We have received a large number of calls for help from accountants, business

8

owners, and insurance agents in similar situations. Don't think this will happen to you. It is happening to a lot of accountants and business owners, because most of these so-called listed, abusive plans, or plans substantially similar to the so-called listed, are currently being sold by most insurance agents.

Bruce was a small business owner facing $400,000 in IRS penalties for 2004 and 2005 for his 412(i) plan (IRC6707A). Here is how the story developed.

In 2002 an insurance agent representing a 100-year-old well-established insurance company suggested he start a pension plan. Bruce was given a portfolio of information from the insurance company, which was given to the company's outside CPA to review and to offer an opinion. The CPA gave the plan the green light and the plan was started for tax year 2002.

Contributions were made in 2003. Then the administrator came out with amendments to the plan, based on new IRS guidelines, in October 2004.

The business owner's agent disappeared in May 2005 before implementing the new guidelines from the administrator with the insurance company. The business owner was left with a refund check from the insurance company, a deduction claim on his 2004 tax return that had not been applied, and without an agent.

It took six months of making calls to the insurance company to get a new insurance agent assigned. By then, the IRS had started an examination of the pension plan. Bruce asked for advice from the CPA and the local attorney (who had no previous experience in such cases), which made matters worse, with a "big name" law firm being recommended and more than $30,000 in additional legal fees being billed in three months.

To make a long story short, the audit stretched on for more than two years to examine a two-year old pension with four participants and $178,000 in contributions.

During the audit, no funds went to the insurance company. The company was awaiting IRS approval on restructuring the plan as a traditional defined benefit plan, which the administrator had suggested and which IRS had indicated would be acceptable. The $90,000 2005 contribution was put into the company's retirement bank account along with the 2004 contribution.

In March 2008, the business owner received an apology from the IRS agent who headed the examination. Even this sympathetic IRS agent thinks there is a problem with the IRS enforcement of these Draconian penalties. Below is one of her e-mails to the business owner who was fined $400,000.

From: XXXXXXXX XXXXX <XXXXXXXX.XXXXX@irs.gov>
Date: Tue, Mar 4, 2008 at 7:12 AM
Subject: RE: Urgent
To: Bruce Hink <brucehink@XXXXXXXX.com>

Thanks Bruce—yes—please just overnight them to the Grand Rapids address. Once again, I'm sorry about this. Basically, our Counsel told us that we needed language specific to the IRC 6707A penalty in order for that statute to be extended. I will ask the Reviewer to hold off an extra day.

I'm also very sorry that this is getting you down. Deeply sorry. It's very difficult for me as well—before I started working this project (412(i)) I was doing audits of 401(k) and profit sharing plans. If there was an error in the plan, the employer would just fix it and the audit was over. There wasn't anything controversial or adversarial about it—and I felt like I was helping people—employers and plan participants. I really liked my job. In two years time, that has completely changed. I know it's not very "professional" to make such confessions—so forgive me. But I guess I just wanted you to know that I really sympathize with your situation—and have been doing whatever I can to help. I know that having this hanging over your head can't be fun—but as this project goes forward—I think that the IRS is going to have to soften their position somewhat—so these delays may be to your benefit.

Also, I'm not really supposed to be sending emails to you—but when I went through the file I couldn't find a good phone number for you. Could you just send me a note or an email with a current phone number?

Looking to receive the signed 872s on Thursday. If you have any questions at any time—please call me at XXX-XXX-XXX. I'm usually in the office in the mornings.

The IRS subsequently denied any appeal and ruled in October 2008 that the $400,000 penalty would stand.

Could You or One of Your Clients Be Next?

Some of the areas SB/SE will be examining include pass-through entities, high-income filers, and abusive transactions. S corporations are likely to receive particular scrutiny. Further review would not be limited to S corporations, but would extend to pass-through entities like partnerships, which can expect to receive a "significant amount of attention" because SB/SE has found an area of abuse and would like to curb what is called a growing trend of abusive transactions. There also will be a renewed effort to address high-income filers, typically classified as those with an adjusted gross income of more than $200,000.

The IRS has been cracking down on what it considers to be abusive tax shelters. Many of them are being marketed to small business owners by insurance professionals, financial planners, and even accountants and attorneys. I speak at numerous conventions, for both business owners and accountants.

And after I speak, I am always approached by many people who have questions about tax reduction plans that they have heard about.

I have been an expert witness in many of these 419 and 412(i) lawsuits and I have not lost one of them. If you sold one or more of these plans, get someone who really knows what they are doing to help you immediately. Many advisors will take your money and claim to be able to help you. Make sure they have experience helping agents that have sold these types of plans. Make sure they have experience helping accountants who signed the tax returns. IRS calls them material advisors and fines them $200,000 if they are incorporated or $100,000 if not. Do not let them learn on the job, with your career and money at stake.

Fear will not adjust your opponent's motive. Strategic action on your part, though, will make your business adept enough to handle adversarial challenges. You need advocates with tax law knowledge who can strategically allocate your business assets, utilizing legal methods synchronized to an understanding of the most recently updated IRS code provisions. You should meet the IRS challenge as an opportunity to advance your business and wealth-growth goals.

Let us discuss an integrated team approach to protecting your assets, a strategy that should be in place long before the IRS, or other vampirical entities seeking to drain your assets appear at the doorstep. Nothing you do as a business owner is as important as understanding how to minimize your risk.

Summary

Macroeconomic conditions have resulted in stupefying losses to the investment portfolios of both the public and private sectors. The country is rife with projected pension fund insolvencies totaling literally hundreds of billions of dollars. Our (read: taxpayers) share is staggering. The government is looking for revenue wherever it can find it. Cue the Internal Revenue Service!

Profound Insight #1

I became confused when I heard these terms with reference to the word "service:"

Internal Revenue Service
U.S. Postal Service
Telephone Service
Cable Service
Civil Service
Customer Service
State, City, and County Public Service

But today, I overheard two farmers talking, and one of them said he had hired a bull to "service" a few cows.

BAM!!! It all came into focus.

Now I understand what all those service agencies are doing to us.

I hope you are as enlightened as I am.

CHAPTER 2

Everyone Needs a Family Office

It's less about the physical training, in the end, than it is about the mental preparation: Boxing is a chess game. You have to be skilled enough and have trained hard enough to know how many different ways you can counterattack in any situation, at any moment.

—Jimmy Smits

One of the truisms that virtually everyone has heard is that "the rich get richer." Why? In the modern era, one answer is that families of great wealth avail themselves of family office structures.

Why a Family Office?

A family office is a comprehensive team of professionals: estate planning attorney, tax attorney, CPA, financial planner, investment advisor, life insurance agent, property and casualty insurance broker, and the family office administrator—all working together to preserve, protect, and perpetuate a family's wealth.

So what is the big deal, you ask? Except for the family office administrator, don't most people with reasonable assets and income employ all these professionals? Not really. Ask yourself: "When is the last time I got my estate planning attorney, tax attorney, CPA, financial planner, investment advisor, life insurance agent, and property and casualty insurance broker all in the same room, working together on a comprehensive plan for me?" The answer for most people is "Never!" As a matter of fact, for most people these professionals have never even spoken to each other, and most of the time, don't even know each other's names.

Why is this so important? Why could having all these professionals meeting on a regular basis be so important to you and your family? There are hundreds of questions that need to be answered every year. Here are a few of them:

- Have you changed your will and your trust since the birth, death, or divorce of a child?

Probably not. Your lawyer doesn't know about the changes, and you're too busy.

- Has your life insurance agent established the lowest-costing insurance available in the market this year, or simply used the company he has a contract with?

Most probably he has a vested interest in selling and maintaining policies with his current company, not finding you the lowest cost among 1,600 life insurance companies.

- Has your CPA run a cost–benefit analysis on your life insurance policies?

Probably not. In a sample series of calls made in researching this article, I could not locate even a single CPA who had ever received a request of this nature.

- Has your property and casualty insurance been requoted every year to minimize the cost of coverage for your autos, homes, businesses, and everything else? Have these coverages been analyzed to make sure that the liability limits are sufficient to trigger your umbrella coverage?

Probably not. In fact, I was unable to find a single person who had ever had this done even once!

- Has anyone ever held your investment advisor's feet to the fire, asking him to justify his selection of investments based on the best returns earned worldwide on those same investment classes?

Probably not. In fact, I was unable to locate a single investment advisor who could even name the top two or three money managers of portfolios similar to those they themselves used for their own clients!

- Does your CPA allocate the time to actually provide significant tax advice each year, or does he simply prepare your tax return and determine the lowest tax bill after 12/31, when it's impossible to make any changes to your financial structure?

Probably the latter.

You could probably ask yourself hundreds of questions like these, and would no doubt arrive at the same answers.

This crucial analysis is virtually never done. But going through this exercise, I am sure you conclude that although this is incredibly important, you would barely know where to start. You could not imagine scheduling all these people into a meeting room and coordinating an all-day meeting watching your advisors justify to each other member of your team the decisions they have made on your behalf.

I am sure you would agree that even scheduling a meeting like this would trigger a flurry of activity by all of these professionals as they scrambled to analyze the actions they had recommended for you, especially when they realize that the rest of the members of your team are going to scrutinize their actions!

A flurry of professional activity on your behalf sounds like a good thing! So why doesn't everyone do this? It is because they are missing a key member on their team. They are missing a family office administrator—a professional who is retained to take on the responsibility of organizing this annual comprehensive review. The very wealthy usually have this professional on their staff.

But the "regular millionaire," the physician, the entrepreneur, and business owner do not know where to turn. They cannot justify the cost of a high-level professional administrator, and would not be able to locate someone with the broad experience to take on this task, even if they could afford it.

Retaining a Firm

So, what can these professionals and business owners do? They can retain a family office management firm—a company in the business of providing this service to hundreds of clients on a shared-cost basis.

One department engages in comprehensive data gathering: building a portfolio of every will, trust, business agreement, set of incorporation papers, insurance policy, and investment, along with detailed personal and corporate financial statements. The portfolio is then transferred to the firm's planning department where their CPAs and attorneys review everything and prepare a list of issues that need to be addressed.

Telephone conferences are then scheduled with each of the client's advisors. The client's attorney, CPA, and so forth, are provided an explanation of the new family office structure being put in place under the direction of the firm. Then a discussion is held on the issues raised by the planning department.

Over a period of several weeks or months, a series of comprehensive changes are arrived at, and an all-day meeting is scheduled with the client and all of his advisors. The new proposed plan is presented and over the course of the day, the client will make his decisions. There is never an issue of "I'd like to check this out with my attorney, CPA, agent, broker, and so on" because all of these people are sitting right in front of him. The firm's client services department then takes over, supervising the implementation of all the agreed-on changes and additions.

The Family Office Advantage

What makes this procedure so efficacious is that it is an annual event, possibly even semi-annual for clients with a great deal of wealth or a lot of activity. And it enables the client to employ a team of high-end professionals at a cost that makes sense.

Once the family office is in place, another important consideration is that most CPAs are simply tax preparers and only incorporate basic planning techniques, if any at all. Firms incorporate advanced, IRS-compliant tax planning strategies that have been used for decades by wealthy families and their advisors, as well as major U.S. corporations, and have made them available to the ordinary millionaire. They work with their client's CPA and investment people to educate them on these strategies. A typical plan might include the following objectives:

- Placing assets in the most effective asset protection vehicles
- Providing a tax-efficient environment in which most investments, including real estate, securities, closely held stock, can experience lower or even zero tax rates
- Providing business owners the ability to use Fortune 500–type strategies to reduce corporate taxation
- Increasing net worth and funds available for retirement through compliant tax planning and to minimize the taxation on these funds when they are withdrawn

Whether you employ a professional family office adminis-trator or do the work yourself, it is essential that all profession-als, businesspeople, and people with reasonable wealth conduct this annual exercise. Implementing the above mentioned advanced tax planning strategies and reducing various tax loads associated with one's pretax income and after-tax invest-ments can literally change the way you live and when you retire. There is probably no more important planning work you can do.

Summary

Lack of coordination among trusted advisors results in loss of planning opportunities, greater tax penalties, decreased asset protection, and decreased wealth accumulation. A family office firm offers planning capabilities to the average investor on a cost-sharing basis that were previously accessible only by ultra-high-net-worth clients. A competent family office firm should be in every trusted advisor's personal "services provided" portfolio.

Profound Insight #2

The United States has come up with a new weapon that destroys people but leaves buildings standing.

It's called the stock market.

CHAPTER 3

Protect Your (Retirement) Assets

All the time he's boxing, he's thinking.
All the time he's thinking, I was hitting him.

—*Jack Dempsey*

The Fiduciary Duty

Government officials now expect 401(k) plan sponsors to conduct periodic due diligence reviews. The problem is that most sponsors (owners) do not have the in-house resources to do so. Historically, this is not something that 401(k) plan sponsors do. On the heels of recent mutual fund scandals, though, Labor Department officials indicated that sponsors had a duty to periodically investigate plans and benchmark funds and fees.

Baby boomers are now retiring, and their 401(k) accounts often are their primary source of retirement income. A sponsor can potentially be held liable for less than stellar 401(k) account growth if employees can demonstrate that the employer did not meet its fiduciary duties.

Trusting the reputation of a major mutual fund company is not enough anymore. Sponsors must investigate and compare their plans to other programs at least every two to five years, as well as demonstrate that their plan expenses are in line with what others are paying. Blind trust is not prudent. You need a process, and you need to document that process.

Documenting a Process

Every fiduciary decision has to be made via a careful process. According to the Employee Retirement Income Security Act (ERISA), the primary plan fiduciary is the sponsor, in other words, the employer. Therefore, it is the employer's responsibility to ensure the prudent selection and oversight of plan vendors.

Sponsors must monitor vendors in two ways:

1. Micro-monitoring, which should occur annually, examines plan features and services.
2. Macro-monitoring every three years or so allows sponsors to benchmark with competitors.

Smaller employers who comparatively lack resources and manpower find it difficult to monitor vendors to this extent. Thus, owing to ERISA provisions that compel bewildered sponsors to take on experts to help with due diligence, most small-to mid-sized plans need to hire consultants.

There is potential liability if due diligence reviews are not conducted. Failure to engage in a prudent process may breach fiduciary duties, which may render the sponsor liable for damages. For example, if plan participants pay fees that are higher than the current market rate because the sponsor did not perform a review, that fiduciary could be liable for the higher fees.

However, as long as the sponsor can prove he did a proper investigation, he can potentially shield himself from liability. The employer has to show that he engaged in a prudent process and that he made a reasonable decision based on that process. This applies to all retirement plans, not only 401(k) plans. Most importantly, not only does the employer have to *perform* these duties, the employer must be able to *document* how the duties were faithfully performed.

Plan Options/Simple IRA

Optimal ways for employers and employees to save for retirement has become one of the biggest employer benefit issues in recent years. If you provide retirement benefits, your benefits plan may have started out simply, then increased in complexity as your business has grown.

Defined benefit plans and 401(k) plans can be expensive to administer and may require significant employer contributions. As the owner of the business, qualified plan rules may limit the amount of money you can save within the plan. These limitations may prevent you from adequately replacing your income in retirement.

What strategy is there for small businesses in this situation?

The SIMPLE IRA and life insurance approach to retirement planning provides the business owner the ability to receive tax benefits during his working years and income during retirement in a two-step process. A SIMPLE IRA is an employer-sponsored plan in which plan contributions are made to a participating employee's IRA.

There are some great advantages to this approach.

First, the SIMPLE IRA provides tax savings now by allowing you to defer income and income taxes until funds are received, typically during retirement. Then, to mitigate the taxes you will have to pay on your retirement income from the SIMPLE IRA, the life insurance policy allows for tax-free distributions. These tax-free distributions increase the ability to maintain the lifestyle you have become accustomed to, from working life through retirement years.

If you are new to the SIMPLE IRA plan design, you must first adopt a SIMPLE IRA plan using one of the many mutual fund family providers of your choice. (It is wise to seek out a plan that offers asset allocation funds for your employees.) The adoption of a retirement plan for your employees is a visible employee benefit proven to increase job satisfaction and retention.

For you as the business owner, SIMPLE IRAs have many advantages, including low maintenance costs, and the ability to maximize your contributions regardless of what your employees defer, as well as providing a match only for the employees who participate in the plan. The match is tax-deductible to you, and no third-party administration is needed—this results in little or no plan costs for the employer, depending on the product you choose.

The costs in a 401(k) plan can run in the thousands of dollars, so many employers prefer to use the SIMPLE IRA plan design.

As long as you have fewer than 100 employees, you are eligible to adopt this plan for your business. The SIMPLE IRA plan allows all assets to grow tax-deferred, maximizing growth. However, deferrals are limited to $10,500 (for 2008), with an extra $2,500 if you are over age 50. The match can be as much as 3 percent of pay up to $10,500 (if you reach that limit, it equates to a $350,000 salary). So, where's the problem?

You Cannot Save Enough

Well, if you are the owner of a firm and you are making a substantial income, deferring $10,500 (even if you can maximize the matching funds) is probably not going to allow you to replace your needed income in retirement. Since most of us do not aspire to a lower standard of living in retirement, you have to save more money outside the plan to maintain your present lifestyle in retirement.

How best to do this?

Remember you are building up a potentially large pool of money that has not been subject to income tax yet, so it is best to hedge that position with an asset that provides both growth and tax-free withdrawals. Using an overfunded life insurance policy is an effective way to accomplish this because the cash values grow tax-deferred within the life insurance contract and withdrawals are income tax-free up to the amount of premiums contributed to the policy.

If the life insurance is structured properly, tax-free withdrawals may be taken for years from the policy. Also, using a life insurance policy allows the owner to save more for retirement without having to provide additional benefits to any of the employees. And the life insurance usually fills an existing need for family protection that is overlooked by small business owners.

So, as you can see, adoption of a SIMPLE IRA retirement plan combined with supplemental life insurance works well for everyone concerned in a small business. The rank and file employees have a matching arrangement that is closely related to a safe harbor 401(k), yet the employer is able to minimize his out-of-pocket contribution. Also, the key personnel can benefit from the life insurance values both now and in the future without concern for ERISA issues. This is indeed a very "simple" and effective arrangement for a small business owner to save for retirement.

Another Option—The 412(e)(3)

Another strategy for businesses with highly taxed owners and few employees is a 412(e)(3) plan. Successful business owners need big deductions and benefits, which can only be accomplished through a defined benefit plan. Any business can use a 412(e)(3) plan to provide benefits and reduce taxes substantially. The 412(e)(3) plan allows the owner to get the largest legal deduction. At 45, an owner can deduct more than $200,000 per year, and more than $300,000 per year at age 55.

Most accountants have never heard of these types of plans, which were defined by the Pension Protection Act of 2006 and are regulated by the IRS and the Department of Labor. The best fit is with companies that have highly taxed owners, but few employees—perfect for doctors, commercial real estate salespeople, consultants, and other small business owners.

A larger business would be better off with a cash balance plan, which also allows owners and key employees to make large contributions. A 412(e)(3) is easy to administer and simple to explain. Other benefits can include asset protection and the ability to deduct life insurance. Care must be taken with respect to who administers the plan.

There have been abuses with the operation of some of these plans and the IRS has disallowed deductions for some abuses. It is important to know with whom you are dealing, and that the administrator has the experience and integrity to run the plan correctly. Just because an insurance company may be involved does not make the operation of the plan legitimate.

There are many benefits to using a 412(e)(3) plan. In addition to the large tax deduction, the plan can even be combined with a 401(k) plan. This may be the ideal tax deduction for the profitable small business owner or professional.

The Cash-Balance Plan

Many profitable small business owners would like to have a retirement plan that can provide more than $50,000 in annual deductible contributions to the owners and other key employees. A defined benefit (DB) plan is perhaps the only tax-qualified retirement plan that can achieve this. However, in traditional DB plans, the worker benefit costs are too high to make them practical. A cash-balance plan is the solution.

Unlike other defined benefit plans, a cash-balance plan may be designed to better control the cost of the rank-and-file employee benefits. A cash-balance plan may be designed to level the owner's contributions, despite wide differences in age (not shown), or to optimize each owner's contribution. The typical cash-balance plan often results in more than 90 percent of the benefits being derived by the business owners.

The cash-balance plan (see Exhibit 3.1) uses an innovative allocation method allowable under the Internal Revenue Code to provide comparable benefits to the owners, when compared to the average benefit awarded to the employees. "Comparable" need not be equal. This ability makes cash-balance plans

Exhibit 3.1   Sample Cash-Balance Plan

Name/Position	Age	Salary	Employer Contribution*
Owner 1	64	$220,000	$239,360
Owner 2	51	220,000	108,240
Worker A	49	70,000	5,040
Worker B	37	65,000	4,680
Worker C	30	62,000	4,464
Worker D	32	60,000	4,320
Worker E	28	56,000	4,032
Worker F	36	30,000	2,160
Worker G	30	25,000	1,800
Worker H	44	25,000	1,800
Worker I	48	22,000	1,585
Worker J	44	20,000	1,440
Worker K	41	20,000	1,440
Worker L	48	15,000	1,080
Worker M	67	12,000	864
Worker N	55	11,000	792
Plan Totals		$933,000	$383,096
Owners Total		$440,000	$347,600
Percent to Owners		47%	91%

*Assumes that the company will maintain its existing 401(k) plan and provide at least a 5% of pay contribution to all non-key employees to satisfy the "top-heavy" minimum requirements of *both* plans under IRC 415.

feasible in many situations where a classic defined benefit plan would be too costly.

Unlike traditional defined benefit plans that are often under-appreciated, a cash-balance plan awards each participant a specific contribution, and the plan guarantees that it will grow at a fixed rate selected by the business owner. The retirement benefit may simply be the cash balance.

Its advantages include:

- Acquiring tax deductible life insurance
- Protecting assets from creditors
- Guaranteed retirement and survivor benefits
- Leveling owner contributions, if desired
- Easy to understand
- Larger plan contributions and tax deductions
- The ability to combine with a 401(k) plan

All of the above methods are a means to control company costs and return value to the owner-investor's wallet.

Summary

There are tax-qualified (read: tax-reducing) plans available to meet the needs of virtually every employer. For the business owner–investor, it is often difficult to evaluate differences in product, service level, and potential rate of return. Finally, the employer must assess the increase, or decrease, in value-added benefit. A financial advisor with the expertise, ability, and desire to properly inform the employer of the available options is a prerequisite for adequate retirement planning.

Profound Insight #3

How do you make a small fortune?
   Start with a large one.

CHAPTER 4

How Much Did You Lose Last Year?

Boxing is the only sport you can get your brain shook, your money took, and your name in the undertaker book...

—*Joe Frazier*

We have already delved into some of the technical procedures available to enhance your business wealth–growth opportunities. This chapter is simple. We step back and look at the overall arc of your business planning by asking 15 pertinent questions. Take the challenge and then take control.

Basic Financial Strategies Quiz

You should be able to answer each question and also to formulate a rationale for that response. Each question itemizes a potential strategic benefit that may be a proper fit for your business and your investment growth needs.

- Do you have a current estate and financial plan?
- Do you have a low-load or no-load life insurance contract?
- Do you have a current business succession plan?
- Do you have a fully funded buyout agreement?
- Have you been paying too much for medical insurance?
- Is your money protected from the claims of potential creditors?

- Is a Voluntary Employee Beneficiary Association (VEBA) plan right for you? (With proper planning a VEBA can make many of the above items tax deductible.)
- Do you think you are paying too much in taxes?
- Have you provided for a secure retirement?
- Has your retirement plan been amended to take advantage of current law changes?
- Do you have a health savings account or, even better, a health-care reimbursement arrangement?
- Is a 412(e)(3) plan right for you?
- Are you doing anything that will trigger an IRS audit?
- Are you currently in any type of plan that the IRS considers to be an abusive tax shelter?
- Are you "renting" a captive insurance company to reduce costs and taxes?

If you cannot answer, do not know the answer, or do not understand the questions in the above checklist, you and your assets are vulnerable. But I bet you know how much you lost last year. Assess your own personal discomfort ratio. How much did you lose last year, compared to how much you *do not* want to lose this year?

These questions are not intended to simply demonstrate what you and your client don't know. They are intended to serve as guideposts. Most clients have failed to take the most basic of precautionary measures to protect themselves from financial ruin, and because most CPAs are ill-equipped to knowledgeably inform their clients about where the client is sorely lacking—we have the potential for disaster. So let us address these issues, quite briefly, one by one.

Estate and Financial Planning

The majority of your clients probably do not have so much as a simple will. Of those clients who do, the majority of *them* have not established a living trust, leaving themselves subject to probate and the resultant possibility of public scrutiny. Consider the percentage of your married clients, facing possible estate taxes, who have not established an A/B trust. The simplest, most basic of estate planning tools are rarely properly utilized. Is it really necessary for me to go into the lack of financial planning among your clientele?

Life Insurance

Most of your clients are not properly covered by their life insurance. Please note: I did not say *adequately* covered. There is a big difference. *Adequately* implies "they need to buy more." *Properly* implies that they may have too much insurance, or the wrong kind, or a policy that is underperforming, or one sold as part of a "retirement plan" that is likely to get them in trouble with the IRS. If you, their CPA, have a life insurance license, *make sure* that you partner with an independent, professional, life insurance specialist who will help ensure you are providing the best possible advice.

Succession Planning

Unfortunately, succession planning is one of those things the business owner just never seems to get around to completing. Whether it is the necessity of contemplating retirement (or demise), of the difficulty in dealing with what are often family issues, it just does not get done. The result, for many business owners, is a failure to fully maximize the value of and capitalize on, what is in all likelihood their greatest financial asset— their business. This is a conversation you need to have with your clients. If you personally do not have the expertise to perform this type of specialized consultative service, find somebody who does.

The Buy-Sell

I cannot tell you how many times I speak with business owners who tell me, "Oh yeah, I have a Buy-Sell agreement in place." When I ask the obvious follow-up question ("How is it funded?"), I am often met with a blank stare. A non–fully funded Buy-Sell is less than worthless. It provides the business owners with a false sense of security. Business owners think they have addressed an issue when they have not. Although a full and complete discussion of Buy-Sell design and funding is beyond the scope of this book, the days of the simple "cross-purchase" agreement *ought* to be over. Sadly, they are not.

Medical Insurance

By the time this book reaches print, one thing is certain. The arguments about health care (and health Insurance) cost-containment will *not* be over. The arguments will never be over. The greatest cost savings and cost-containment measures for the business owner can be achieved only through expert plan design. The difficulty lies in the fact that the typical benefits broker is expert at only one thing—selling the prepackaged solution offered by their favored provider to maximize the broker's own commission. It is incumbent on a trusted advisor to steer the client toward someone with both the expertise and the willingness to offer cutting-edge solutions to the client.

Asset Protection

Creditors come in many guises, not simply in the form of a lawsuit. That having been said, plaintiffs, the IRS, and the vagaries of the stock market, pose what are likely the three biggest dangers to your client's assets. All three are easily mitigated, provided the proper advance planning is utilized. This is another of those areas where a CPA is simply not trained to take advantage of the latest in asset protection strategies. Consult a competent advisor. Do you detect a theme yet?

VEBA

According to the IRS, VEBA is an acronym for "voluntary employee beneficiary association." VEBAs are trusts that are exempt from tax under the provisions of IRC section 501(c)(9). A VEBA is a "welfare benefit fund" to which sections 419 and 419A will apply if it is part of an employer's plan through which the employer provides welfare benefits to employees and their beneficiaries. Although welfare benefit funds can also be taxable trusts, most welfare benefit funds apply for exempt status as VEBAs in order to reduce or eliminate income taxes at the trust level. VEBAs file Form 990; taxable trusts file Form 1041.

A "welfare benefit" is an employee benefit other than those to which IRC sections 83(h), 404, and 404A apply. The most common types of welfare benefits are medical, dental, disability, severance, and life insurance benefits.

Properly structured VEBAs can therefore serve as tax-favored funding vehicles for many of the foreseeable expenditures (benefits obligations) a business owner is likely to incur.

Other Post-Employment Benefits

In 1994 the Government Accounting Standards Board (GASB) established standards for public employee pension plans. Government and public employers have to report and account for pension benefits costs. However, until recent years there was no such standard in place for other post-employment benefits (OPEBs) for state and local government workers. Private sector employers have been required to report OPEBs for more than 15 years under the FASB Standards 106/158.

Government and public sector employers have been required to report OPEBs since August 2004 after the issuance of GASB Statement 45. This means that all government employers must now keep their promise of providing retiree benefits. Benefits need to be calculated accurately, accrued during the employee's years of work with the employer, and recognized as a financial obligation as OPEB costs. These costs are to be reported on financial statements of large public sector employers beginning with the first financial report period after December 15, 2006, and on small employers beginning in 2008.

The intent of GASB 45 was to bring government and public accounting standards in line with private company standards. This requires reporting pensions as well as nonpension post-employment benefits. As the name states, OPEBs are benefits other than pensions. Many state and local governments, public schools, public universities, and other public and government agencies provide post-employment benefits that are nonpension-related. These benefits can include health-care benefits such as vision, dental, prescription and health insurance; life insurance; legal benefits and other nonpension-related work benefits.

Until these changes were put in place with GASB 45 and enforced, readers of government and public financial statements had incomplete information on the costs of services provided by state and local governments and public employers, and were therefore unable to analyze the financial position and long-term health of these government and public agencies.

OPEB Cost

Actuarial calculations are used to derive the OPEB cost. In order to keep the calculations up-to-date, they must be recalculated every two to three years depending on the size of the employer. For example, employers with less than 100 employees can use a simplified alternative method for measuring the OPEB cost, but these employers still need to reevaluate and reassess every three years. The costs and obligations for post-employment benefits are determined by using the actuarial present value of the post-employment benefits—in other words, the present value on term of service and the terms of the OPEB plan that are presently in place.

Assumptions that are made in the actuarial evaluations include:

- Health-care cost factors: age, industry, family, geography, gender
- Expected long-term and/or short-term rate of return on plan assets
- Projected salary scale
- Death rates
- Projected inflation of medical care costs
- Employee turnover rate
- Retirement rates; this can vary extensively from year to year
- Any promises made to retirees
- Discounts or benefits designed into the plan

After the actuarial evaluations are completed, each employee gains a different attribution period, which is based on their period of eligibility—date of hire to date of full eligibility (i.e., retirement). With all this said, GASB only requires that employers report OPEBs; employers are not required or even obligated to fund the OPEB cost. However, not doing so can affect significantly an employer's credit rating and cost of issuing debt financing.

The largest OPEB cost for an employer is health-care benefits. The majority of public sector employers with more than 200 employees offer some form of post-employment health benefits. Unfortunately, with the uncontrollable increases in health-care costs happening annually, and severe budget cuts being put in place across nearly all public and government agencies, the continuing use of "pay-as-you-go" will become more difficult and create new financial liabilities for employers. Add to this state laws that require employers to allow retirees to remain on the active health plan until Medicare steps in, and the reduction in federal and state subsidies, and employers are struggling to subsidize the gap between the blended plan cost (active employees and retirees) and the actual retiree cost. Even if the employer is not contributing to the retiree health-care plan, this amount adds additional liability.

In December 2004, a report from Standard & Poor's stated that:

> *The new [GASB 45] reporting may reveal cases in which the actuarial funding of post-employment health benefits would seriously strain operations, or, further, may uncover conditions under which employers are unable or unwilling to fulfill these obligations. In such cases, these liabilities may adversely affect the employer's creditworthiness. All Standard & Poor's rated employers will be monitored closely in terms of their reporting under GASB 45. Upon implementation of these new standards, we will include the new information as part of our ongoing analytical surveillance of ratings.*

In June 2005 Fitch Ratings released its report, saying: "Fitch's credit focus will be on understanding each issuer's [GASB 45] liability and its plans for addressing it. Fitch also will review an entity's reasoning for developing its plan. An absence of action taken to fund OPEB liabilities or otherwise manage them will be viewed as a negative rating factor. Steady progress toward reaching the actuarially determined annual contribution level will be critical to sound credit quality."

Everyone is working toward a solution that will benefit both employers and employees, but it takes constant monitoring by both employers and employees. However, one solution merits consideration from everyone is implementing a VEBA plan.

VEBA Plan Benefits

VEBAs have been successfully established to help reduce health costs and establish financially sound OPEB plans that have proven to be both efficient and effective. The VEBA can help employers develop strategies that can lower their liabilities. Many private sector employers have benefited from the introduction and use of a VEBA for their OPEB plan.

A well-designed GASB 45 OPEB involves many different risk-management strategies and funding techniques. Any benefit promise made by an employer should be partially or fully funded in a qualified trust to enable actuaries the use of long-term discount rates during the calculations. One approach to this funding source could be issuing OPEB obligation bonds or finance pools. The employer can then successfully take these finance strategies and blend a defined-benefit approach with a defined-contribution strategy to create a successfully managed OPEB plan with reduced liabilities. These two basic forms of post-employment benefit plans specify either the amount of benefits to be provided to an employee at the end of their employment period, or stipulate only the amount to be contributed by the employer to a member's account for each year of active employment.

A defined-benefit OPEB plan is where the terms are specified and the benefits provided from the time of retirement or other employment separation. These benefits can be dollar-specific or the type/level of coverage—for example, a dollar payment based on a flat rate or years of service, or defined medical coverage, prescription drugs, or a percentage of the premiums. Unfortunately, the defined benefit OPEB plan is complicated where the reporting makes assumptions on future medical costs, mortality rates, the availability of Medicare, and the probability of future events.

A defined-contribution OPEB plan considers the individual. It takes into account individual contributions while active, rather than the benefits the beneficiaries are to receive post-employment. Benefits for the defined-contribution plan consist of contributions, earnings on investments of these contributions, and forfeitures on the member's account. This makes the plan easier to report on, but does not specify the amount of benefits received by the employee after retirement.

GASB accrual standards only apply to defined-benefit OPEB plans. Defined contributions are considered "funded," because the employer cost equals the required contribution. Therefore, changing the way retiree health care and other post-employment benefits are paid can lower or even eliminate the unfunded other post-employment benefits liability.

Now that the public sector and government agencies have to report other post-employment benefits, the VEBA can establish the best plan for the least liability for employers. State and local governments and public services can look at the private sector and see the benefits it has gained from using VEBAs. They can see how it can help soften the financial impact of the new, significant reporting obligation.

Taxes

Many CPAs are more proficient at ensuring that the proper amount of taxes are paid in any given situation than they are at helping to establish a situation where the properly minimized amount of taxes is being paid. No citizen is compelled to pay more taxes than are legally required, and every citizen may order their affairs in such a fashion that their tax obligation is minimized. The full panoply of available tax reduction methodologies would fill several textbooks. If you, as a CPA, are not at least conceptually familiar with the basics of the various business structures, retirement plan designs, and captive insurance companies, your clients are ill-served unless you help them find somebody who is.

Retirement

As currently structured, the Cash-Balance Defined Benefit Plan is likely to allow key employees the best combination of tax-deferral and high contribution limits. The problem is that plan design and administration can be somewhat burdensome. 401(k)/profit-sharing combinations are relatively straightforward, but fail the "how much money can the key employees stuff in" test as a result of their comparatively low contribution limits. More advanced Buy-Sell strategies, which leverage corporate tax rates and result in subsidized contributions to the key employees, are helpful—but not a stand-alone solution. Generally, some combination of the three approaches, or the incorporation of more "esoteric" design strategies is necessary for the highly compensated businessperson.

Legislative Changes

A competent TPA (Third Party Administrator) can be depended on to make the requisite changes to the plan document in order to comply with (and take advantage of) recent federal legislative changes. Sadly, not every TPA can be relied on to demonstrate that level of competence.

HSA/HRA

The Health Savings Account has proven particularly useful as a tool to help lower the ever-increasing cost of health insurance premiums. When established early enough, HSAs can ultimately serve as a quite useful pool of funds to help defray the cost of medical care in retirement. Health-care reimbursement arrangements provide the business owner with even more leverage to contain health-care costs.

412(e)

Any business can use a 412(e)(3) to provide benefits and reduce taxes substantially. Most accountants have never heard of these types of plans, which were designated by the Pension Protection Act of 2006 and authorized by the IRS and the Department of Labor. The best fit is with companies that have highly taxed owners, but few employees, such as doctors, commercial real estate salespeople, consultants, and other small business owners. Other benefits can include asset protection and the ability to deduct life insurance.

Care must be taken with respect to who administers the plan. There have been abuses with the operation of some of these plans and the IRS has disallowed deductions for some abuses. It is important to know whom you are dealing with and that the administrator has the experience and integrity to run the plan correctly. An insurance company may be involved, but this does not make the operation of the plan legitimate.

Audits

Even in this regulatory/budgetary environment, IRS audits are *not* simply a "fact of life." The tax practitioner must remain keenly aware of likely audit triggers, and scrupulously avoid them unless prepared to mount a vigorous defense supported by scrupulous documentation. Clients often enter into seemingly benign transactions, often at the behest of an insurance salesperson, which can trigger liability on the part of both the client and the CPA if the tax advisor unwittingly signs off on such a plan. Which brings us to…

412(i) Retirement Plans

The IRS has been auditing participants in 412(i) retirement plans. Although there is generally nothing wrong with many of the newer plans, the IRS considered most of the older abusive plans. Forms 8918 and 8886 are also required for abusive 412(i) plans.

Do not wait for IRS to come and get you, or for your client to sue you. Time is of the essence. Most insurance professionals and accountants need help to correct their improperly completed Form 8918 or to fill it out properly in the first place. If you have not previously filled out the form and it is late, you should immediately seek assistance. There are plenty of legitimate tax reduction insurance plans out there. Just make sure that you know the history of the people with whom you conduct business.

Shelters

Many of the listed transactions that can get your clients into trouble with the IRS are exotic shelters that relatively few practitioners ever encounter. When was the last time you saw someone file a return as a Guamanian trust (Notice 2000–61)? On the other hand, a few listed transactions concern relatively common employee benefit plans the IRS has deemed tax-avoidance schemes or otherwise abusive. Perhaps some of the most likely to crop up, especially in small business returns, are arrangements purporting to allow deductibility of premiums paid for life insurance under a welfare benefit plan.

Some of these abusive employee benefit plans are represented as satisfying section 419 of the Code, which sets limits on purposes and balances of "qualified asset accounts" for such benefits, but purport to offer deductibility of contributions without any corresponding income. Others attempt to take advantage of exceptions to qualified asset account limits, such as sham union plans that try to exploit the exception for separate welfare benefit funds under collective-bargaining agreements provided by IRC § 419A(f)(5). Others try to take advantage of exceptions for plans serving 10 or more employers, once popular under section 419A(f)(6). Recently, one may encounter plans relying on section 419(e) and, perhaps, defined-benefit pension plans established pursuant to the former section 412(i) (still so-called, even though the subsection has since been redesignated section 412(e)(3)).

Regardless, the tax practitioner must "handle with care" lest they become personally, professionally, and financially liable. The IRS may call you a material advisor and fine you $200,000. The IRS may fine your clients more than a million dollars for being in a retirement plan, 419 plan, and so forth. As you read this, hundreds of unfortunate people are having their lives ruined by these fines. You may need to take action immediately.

419 Tax-Reduction Insurance Plans

These plans come in various versions, and most of them have or will get the participant audited and the salesperson sued. They purportedly allow the business owner to make a large tax-deductible contribution, and some or all of the contribution pays for a life insurance product. The IRS has been disallowing most versions of these plans for years, yet they continue to be sold. After everyone gets into trouble and the insurance agents and accountants get sued, the promoters of the abusive versions sometimes change the name of their company and call the plan something else. The insurance companies whose policies are sold are legitimate companies.

What usually is not legitimate is the way that most of the plans are operated. There can also be a $200,000 IRS fine facing the insurance agent who sold the plan if Form 8918 has not been properly filed. The accountant who signs the tax return is also fined. I have reviewed hundreds of these forms for agents and accountant and have yet to see one that was filled out correctly.

When the IRS audits a participant in one of these plans, the tax deductions are lost. There is also the interest and large penalties to consider. The business owner can also be facing a $200,000-a-year fine if he did not properly file Form 8886. Most of these forms have been filled out improperly. In my talks with the IRS, I was told that the IRS considers not filling out Form 8886 properly almost the same as not filing at all.

6707A

Internal Revenue Code 6707A was enacted as part of the American Jobs Creation Act on October 22, 2004. It imposes a strict liability penalty for any person who failed to disclose either a listed transaction or reportable transaction per each occurrence. Reportable transactions usually fall within certain general types of transactions (e.g., confidential transactions, transactions with tax protection, certain loss-generating transaction and transactions of interest arbitrarily so designated as by the IRS) that have the potential for tax avoidance. Listed transactions are specified transactions that have been publicly designated by the IRS, including anything that is substantially similar to such a transaction (a phrase that is given liberal construction by the IRS). There are currently 34 listed transactions, including certain retirement plans under Code section 412(i) and certain employee welfare benefit plans funded in part with life insurance under Code sections 419A(f)(5), 419(f)(6), and 419(e). Many of these plans were implemented by small businesses seeking to provide retirement income or health benefits to their employees.

Currently, the IRS has the discretion to assess hundreds of thousands of dollars in penalties under section 6707A of the Code in an attempt to curb tax avoidance shelters. This discretion can be applied regardless of the innocence of the taxpayer and was granted by Congress. If the IRS determines you have engaged in a listed transaction and failed to properly disclose it, you will be subject to a penalty regardless of any other facts and circumstances concerning the transaction. For some, this penalty has been assessed at a million dollars, and for many it is the beginning of a long nightmare.

The IRS may call you a material advisor and fine you $200,000.00. The IRS may fine your clients over a million dollars for being in a retirement plan, a 419 plan, etc. Hundreds of unfortunate people are having their lives ruined by these fines. You may need to take action immediately. As this book went to press, the IRS said it would extend to the end of the year, 2009, the grace period granted to small business owners for collection of certain tax shelter penalties. Congress had not yet acted on the tax shelter penalty legislation. IRS Commissioner Doug Shulman said in a letter to the chairmen and ranking members of tax-writing committees that the IRS would continue to suspend its collection efforts with regard to the penalties until Dec. 31, 2009.

"Clearly, a number of taxpayers have been caught in a penalty regime that the legislation did not intend," wrote Shulman. "I understand that Congress is still considering this issue, and that a bipartisan, bicameral, bill may be in the works."

The issue relates to penalties for so-called listed transactions, the kinds of tax shelters the IRS has designated most egregious. A number of small business owners that bought employee retirement plans, so called 419 and 412(i) plans and others, that were listed by the IRS, and who are now facing hundreds and thousands in penalties, contend that the penalty amounts are unfair.

Leaders of tax-writing committees in the House and Senate have said they intend to pass legislation revising the penalty structure. The IRS has suspended collection efforts in cases where the tax benefit derived from the listed transaction was less than $100,000 for individuals or less than $200,000 for firms.

Senator Ben Nelson (D-Nebraska) has sponsored legislation (S.765) to curtail the IRS and its nearly unlimited authority and power under Code Section 6707A. The bill seeks to scale back the scope of the Section 6707A reportable/listed transaction nondisclosure penalty to a more reasonable level. The current law provides for penalties that are Draconian by nature and offer no flexibility to the IRS to reduce or abate the imposition of the 6707A penalty. This has served as a weapon of mass destruction for the IRS and has hit many small businesses and their owners with unconscionable results. If the new bill passes, large penalties will still be assessed. The penalties, however, will more realistically relate to the deductions taken.

Strict liability requires the IRS to impose the 6707A penalty regardless of innocence of a person (i.e., whether the person knew that the transaction needed to be reported or whether the person made a good faith effort to report) or the level of the person's reliance on professional advisors. A Section 6707A penalty is imposed when the transaction becomes a reportable/listed transaction. Therefore, a person has the burden to keep up-to-date on all transactions requiring disclosure by the IRS into perpetuity for transactions entered into the past.

Additionally, the 6707A penalty strictly penalizes nondisclosure irrespective of taxes owed. Accordingly, the penalty will be assessed even in legitimate tax planning situations when no additional tax is due but an IRS required filing was not properly and timely filed. It is worth noting that a failure to disclose in the view of the IRS encompasses both a failure to file the proper form as well as a failure to include sufficient information as to the nature and facts concerning the transaction. Hence, people may find themselves subject to the 6707A penalty if the IRS determines that a filing did not contain enough information on the transaction. A penalty is also imposed when a person does not file the required duplicate copy with a separate IRS office in addition to filing the required copy with the tax return.

The imposition of a 6707A penalty is not subject to judicial review regardless of whether the penalty is imposed for a listed or reportable transaction. The IRS's determination is conclusive, binding, and final. The next step from the IRS is sending your file to collection, where your assets may be forcibly taken, publicly recorded liens may be placed against your property, and/or garnishment of your wages or business profits may occur, among other measures.

The 6707A penalty amount for each listed transaction is generally $200,000 per year per each person who is not an individual and $100,000 per year per individual who failed to properly disclose each listed transaction. The 6707A penalty amount for each reportable transaction is generally $50,000 per year for each person who is not an individual and $10,000 per year per each individual who failed to properly disclose each reportable transaction. The IRS is obligated to impose the listed transaction penalty by law and cannot remove the penalty by law. The IRS is obligated to impose the reportable transaction penalty by law, as well, but may remove the penalty when the IRS determines that removal of the penalty would promote compliance and support effective tax administration.

The 6707A penalty is particularly harmful in the small business context, where many business owners operate through an

S corporation or limited liability company in order to provide liability protection to the owner-operators. Numerous cases are coming to light where the IRS is imposing a $200,000 penalty at the entity level and then imposing a $100,000 penalty per individual shareholder or member per year.

The individuals are generally left with one of two options:

1. Declare bankruptcy
2. Face a $300,000 penalty per year

Keep in mind, taxes do not need to be due nor does the transaction have to be proven illegal or illegitimate for this penalty to apply. The only proof required by the IRS is that the person did not properly and timely disclose a transaction that the IRS believes the person should have disclosed. It is important to note in this context that for nondisclosed listed transactions, the Statue of Limitations does not begin until a proper disclosure is filed with the IRS.

Many practitioners believe the scope and authority given to the IRS under 6707A, which allows the IRS to act as judge, jury, and executioner, is unconstitutional. Numerous real-life stories abound illustrating the punitive nature of the 6707A penalty and its application to small businesses and their owners. In one case, the IRS demanded that the business and its owner pay a 6707A total of $600,000 for his and his business's participation in a Code section 412(i) plan. The actual taxes and interest on the transaction, assuming the IRS was correct in its determination that the tax benefits were not allowable, was $60,000. Regardless of the IRS's ultimate determination as to the legality of the underlying 412(i) transaction, the $600,000 was due as the IRS's determination was final and absolute with respect to the 6707A penalty. Another case involved a taxpayer who was a dentist and his wife whom the IRS determined had engaged in a listed transaction with respect to a limited liability company. The IRS determined that the couple owed taxes on the transaction of $6,812, since the tax benefits of the transactions were not allowable. In addition, the IRS determined that the taxpayers owed a $1,200,000 section 6707A penalty for both their individual nondisclosure of the transaction along with the nondisclosure by the limited liability company.

Even the IRS personnel continue to question both the legality and the fairness of the IRS's imposition of 6707A penalties. An IRS appeals officer in an e-mail to a senior attorney within the IRS wrote that "…I am both an attorney and CPA and in my 29 years with the IRS I have never [before] worked a case or issue that left me questioning whether in good conscience I could uphold the Government's position even though it is supported by the language of the law." The Taxpayers Advocate, an office within the IRS, even went so far as to publicly assert that the 6707A should be modified as it "raises significant Constitutional concerns, including possible violations of the Eighth Amendment's prohibition against excessive government fines, and due process protection."

Senate bill 765, sponsored by Senator Nelson, seeks to alleviate some of above cited concerns. Specifically, the bill makes three major changes to the current version of Code section 6707A. The bill would allow an IRS-imposed 6707A penalty for nondisclosure of a listed transaction to be rescinded if a taxpayer's failure to file was due to reasonable cause and not willful neglect.

The bill would make a 6707A penalty proportional to an understatement of any tax due. It is my opinion that some legislation will pass. The legislation will have fines for non-disclosure. The fines will be more reasonable, but will still be large, in the range of $10,000 or more. Accordingly, nontax-paying entities such as S corporations and limited liability companies would not be subject to a 6707A penalty (individuals, C corporations, and certain trusts and estates would remain subject to the 6707A penalty).

There are a number of interesting points to note about this action:

1. In the letter, the IRS acknowledges that, in certain cases, the penalty imposed by section 6707A for failure to report participation in a "listed transaction" is disproportionate to the tax benefits obtained by the transaction.
2. In the letter, the IRS says that it is taking this action because Congress has indicated its intention to amend the Code to modify the penalty provision, so that the penalty for failure to disclose will be more in line with the tax benefits resulting from a listed transaction.
3. The IRS will not suspend audits or collection efforts in appropriate cases. It cannot suspend imposition of the penalty, because, at least with respect to listed transactions, it does not have the discretion to not impose the penalty. It is simply suspending collection efforts in cases where the tax benefits are below the penalty threshold in order to give Congress time to amend the penalty provision, as Congress has indicated to the IRS it intends to do.

It should also be noted that identical bills have been introduced in the Senate and the House to amend Section 6707A. Each bill has been referred to the appropriate committee, where no action has taken place. Here are a few points about the proposed legislation:

1. The legislation would reduce the penalty for failure to disclose participation in a reportable transaction, other than a listed transaction, to the amount imposed by section 6662A for an understatement of tax. For a listed transaction, the penalty would equal 200 percent of the penalty imposed

for an understatement of tax. The amount of the penalty imposed by section 6662A is 20 percent.

2. The proposed legislation is different than the position expressed by the IRS. The IRS would like the penalty to equal the tax benefits obtained from the transaction.

3. The legislation does not change the penalty provisions for material advisors. For example, an accountant, who signed a tax return and got paid, would still face a large fine. An insurance agent, who sold one of these plans, would still face a large fine.

Captives

In Chapter 5 we look at one of the most recent popular strategies for managing company benefit cost control—Captive Insurance. The smart strategist understands captive insurance's pitfalls—the flags the IRS researches pre-audit—and the potential benefit of the insurance package when legally and strategically managed.

Summary

Many business owners not only are unaware of the various techniques they can use to protect and grow their assets, they don't even know what they don't know. Knowing what questions to ask is the first step toward gaining the necessary information. Although the questions outlined in this chapter are a good start, they are only that. Inquisitiveness is a vital trait.

Profound Insight #4

How can you double your money?
  Look at it in a mirror.

CHAPTER 5

Self-Defense

Herol Graham has turned defensive boxing into a poetic art. Trouble is, nobody ever got knocked out by a poem.

—Eddie Shaw

E very accountant knows that increased cash flow and cost savings are critical business success factors. What is uncertain is the best path to recommend to garner these benefits.

Over the past decade business owners have been overwhelmed by a plethora of choices designed to reduce the cost of providing employee benefits while increasing their own retirement savings. The solutions range from traditional pension and profit sharing plans to more advanced strategies.

Some strategies, such as IRS section 419 and 412(i) plans, used life insurance as vehicles to bring about benefits. Unfortunately, the high life insurance commissions (often 90 percent of the contribution, or more) fostered an environment that led to aggressive and noncompliant plans.

The result has been thousands of audits and an IRS task force seeking out tax shelter promotion. For unknowing clients, the tax consequences are enormous. For their accountant advisors, the liability may be equally extreme.

Captive Insurance

Recently, there has been an explosion in the marketing of a financial product called Captive Insurance. Small companies have been copying a method to control insurance costs and reduce taxes that used to be the domain of large businesses: setting up their own insurance companies to provide coverage when they think that outside insurers are charging too much. A captive insurance company would be an insurance subsidiary that is owned by its parent business(es). There are now nearly 5,000 captive insurers worldwide. More than 80 percent of Fortune 500 companies take advantage of some sort of captive insurance company arrangement. Now small companies can, too.

These so-called "Captives" are typically small insurance companies designed to insure the risks of an individual business under IRS code section 831(b). When properly designed, a business can make tax-deductible premium payments to a related-party insurance company. Depending on circumstances, underwriting profits, if any, can be paid out to the owners as dividends, and profits from liquidation of the company may be taxed as capital gains. Single-parent captives allow an organization to cover any risk they wish to fund, and generally eliminate the commission-price component from the premiums. Jurisdictions in the United States and in certain parts of the world have adopted a series of laws and regulations that allow small non–life insurance companies, taxed under IRC Section 831(b), or as 831(b) companies.

Basics

Here's how captive insurers work. The parent business (your client's company) creates a captive so that it has a self-funded option for buying insurance, whereby the parent provides the reserves to back the policies. The captive then either retains

52

that risk or pays reinsurers to take it. The price for coverage is set by the parent business; reinsurance costs, if any, are a factor. In the event of a loss, the business pays claims from its captive, or the reinsurer pays the captive. Captives are overseen by corporate boards and, to keep costs low, are often based in places where there is favorable tax treatment and less onerous regulation—such as Bermuda and the Cayman Islands, or U.S. states like Vermont and South Carolina.

Captives have become popular risk-financing tools that provide maximum flexibility to any risk management program. The additional possibility of adding several types of employee benefits is of further strategic value to the owners of captives. Although the employee benefit aspects have not emerged as quickly as had been predicted, there is little doubt that widespread use of captives for employee benefits is just a matter of time. Coverage like long-term disability and term life insurance typically require Department of Labor approval, but other benefit-related coverage such as medical stop-loss can utilize a captive without the department's approval. Additionally, some mid-sized corporate owners also view a captive as an integral part of their asset protection and wealth accumulation plans. The opportunities offered by a captive play a critical role in the strategic planning of many corporations.

A true captive insurance arrangement is where a parent company or some companies in the same economic family (related parties), pay a subsidiary or another member of the family, established as a licensed type of insurance company, premiums that cover the parent company. In theory, underwriting profits from the subsidiary are retained by the parent.

Sharing

There are a number of significant advantages that can be obtained through sharing a large captive with other companies.

The most important is that you can significantly decrease the cost of insurance through this arrangement. By sharing a large captive, participants are insured under group policies, which provide for insurance coverage that recognizes superior claims experience (in the form of experience-rated refunds of premiums) and other profit-sharing options made available to the insured. The second advantage is that sharing a captive does not require any capital commitment and has low policy fees.

The policy application process is similar to that of any commercial insurance company, is relatively straightforward, and aside from an independent actuarial and underwriting review, bears no additional charges. By sharing a captive, you only pay a pro rata fee to cover all general and administrative expenses. The cost for administration is low per insured (historically under 60 basis points annually). By sharing a large captive, loans to its insureds (your company) can be legally made. So you can make a tax-deductible contribution, and then take back money tax-free. Sharing a large captive requires little or no maintenance by the insured and can be implemented in a fraction of the time required for stand-alone captives. If done correctly, sharing a large captive can yield a small company significant tax and cost savings. If done incorrectly, the results can be disastrous. Buyer beware!

Stand-alone captives are also likely to draw IRS attention. Another advantage of sharing a captive is that IRS problems are less likely if that path is followed, and they can be entirely eliminated as even a possibility by following the technique of renting a captive, which would involve no ownership interest in the captive on the part of the insured (your company).

Caveats

Captives can be a great cost-saving tool, but they can also be expensive to build and manage. Also, captives are allowed to garner tax benefits because they operate as real insurance companies. Advisors and business owners who misuse captives or market them as estate planning tools, asset protection or tax deferral vehicles, or other benefits not related to the true business purpose of an insurance company, face grave regulatory and tax consequences.

A recent concern is the integration of small captives with life insurance policies. Small captives under section 831(b) have no statutory authority to deduct life premiums. Also, if a small captive uses life insurance as an investment, the cash value of the life policy can be taxable at corporate rates, and then will be taxable again when distributed. The consequence of this double taxation is to devastate the efficacy of the life insurance, and it extends serious liability to any accountant who recommends the plan or even signs the tax return of the business that pays premiums to the captive.

The IRS is aware that several large insurance companies are promoting their life insurance policies as investments within small captives. The outcome looks eerily like that of the 419 and 412(i) plans mentioned above.

Remember, if something looks too good to be true, it usually is. There are safe and conservative ways to use captive insurance structures to lower costs and obtain benefits for businesses. Some types of captive insurance products do have statutory protection for deducting life insurance premiums (although not 831(b) captives). Learning what works and is safe is the first step an accountant should take in helping his or her clients use these powerful, but highly technical insurance tools.

Summary

Captive insurance companies are one of the more sophisticated cost-savings vehicles available to the small business owner. The benefits of such a vehicle are compelling, rigorous due diligence is necessary *prior* to implementation in order to pass the careful IRS scrutiny, which will almost assuredly follow. If something sounds too good to be true, it undoubtedly is. Make sure that your captive consultant has both the ability and the experience to advise you fully and accurately.

Profound Insight #5

What happened when the cat swallowed a coin?

There was money in the kitty.

CHAPTER 6

Asset Protection Basics

If you screw up in tennis, it's 15-love. If you screw up in boxing, it's your ass.

—Randall "Tex" Cobb

Asset Protection—Necessity, Not Luxury

Asset protection refers to protection of individuals and businesses from civil judgments by using methods, systems, techniques, and procedures developed from statutory law (regulated by Congress or state legislatures) and common law (based on court decisions). Asset protection planning is a strategic, preemptive preparation to prevent creditors from obtaining assets in the event of a civil judgment. It does not mean that a person ignores his debt obligations. It means that a person will control his debt obligations.

True asset protection plans are all encompassing, as opposed to protecting a single asset such as your home. Though it is good to protect a single asset, one must keep in mind "flow-through" liability. Liability can be passed or transferred just as proceeds, profits, and cash revenue can be passed and transferred.

Personal liability is different from business liability, but it is possible to mix the two. However, it is also possible to compartmentalize or separate liabilities and this is a main objective of asset protection plans. A skilled planner will understand the options available for specific circumstances.

Often it is beneficial to go offshore, which may increase security and privacy, in addition to providing interesting planning opportunities, such as greater rates of return on investments and asset protection. All of these considerations are built into an asset protection plan.

Who Needs Asset Protection?

The emotional hurdle is whether you think you need asset protection. The first question is: Do you own anything? If you do, you are someone who should understand the basics. This is the reason we have provided this educational and informative guide.

Whether you need asset protection depends on whether you own any assets. If you do, you are vulnerable to many of the potential entities, such as creditors and judgments that can potentially attack your assets. It was once thought that only the rich needed to protect their assets. New tools and techniques are available and are widely used in estate planning, through insurance products and pension, and so forth, to practice asset protection.

It is a simple fact that 9 out of 10 lawsuits filed and litigated in the world occur in the United States.

If you have assets, you are most likely a target. When your assets are visible, you are the bull's eye. You and your belongings are what litigators refer to as "deep pockets." Even if you create a stealth lifestyle, your assets are discoverable by a motivated creditor.

The core goal of asset protection is to set up your business affairs in such a way that it raises the bar for the professional takers. Your asset protection plan is a proactive step in performing self-help tort reform. You will control your assets and your life, instead of the courts.

Asset protection does not give you the authority to commit fraud or engage in illegal behavior. There is a legal strategy and systematic planning that occurs when you protect your assets from creditors. This plan is specific to your assets and your financial situation and must comply with the IRS and the law.

With asset protection planning, you organize your business and personal affairs in advance of duress, in order to reduce or eliminate liability exposure or financial misfortune by placing assets beyond the reach of future creditors. Asset protection planning has also become a full-grown subspecialty of estate planning.

Asset protection planning is a science and as in all areas of science, there are ethical issues.

- Science—any systematic knowledge or practice
- Ethics—a set of principles or moral conduct

The roots of asset protection are founded in debtor-creditor law. The goal is to remove the assets from the legal title and ownership of the debtor while the debtor retains control and beneficial enjoyment of the assets.

An asset protection plan should change the financial face of the client so that creditors have a more difficult time attaching and seizing the assets, making negotiations favorable to the debtor. A properly constructed asset protection plan also allows the debtor to answer honestly in the face of a judge in court.

The goal is not to avoid debts; the goal is to control debts and settlements.

The word "debtor" may scare you or bring negative connotations at this time because your debts are currently paid. Not only is this understood, but also it is the most beneficial time to protect your assets. The word debtor refers a person in a "post" state of affairs as the accused or judged; in your current state you may have no creditors.

However, there are assumable risks that you take for granted.

Separating Ownership from Control

An American legend and tycoon of the 1930s and 1940s, John D. Rockefeller believed that you should minimize your risk by owning nothing, but controlling everything. This American icon set a standard for preserving wealth and protecting assets. Over the years, a field of law emerged mainstreaming its way into debtor-creditor courts and establishing a basis in statutory law.

Literally, thousands of techniques have evolved for separating ownership (or title) from control and beneficial enjoyment. Every asset had a best way for protection depending on the type of asset, the financial control over the asset and the situation of the owner of the asset. The possibility of a creditor attacking the asset depends on the availability and ease necessary for the seizure and the aggressiveness and intelligence of the creditor.

Protecting assets falls into general philosophies. These philosophies include transferring ownership by way of person or trust, encumbering the property financially, and recording a naked deed of trust, selling assets under long-term contract. The objective is to choose real protection rather than to set up a smoke screen.

Assets must be protected before there are any claims by creditors otherwise the creditor may claim a fraudulent transfer of assets.

What Is an Asset Protection Plan?

Every plan is different, but every plan must fit within the statutory framework and within the assets and their needs.

First, the planner must identify and quantify the risk of the client. Then the planner must analyze the asset and the structures available for that asset. The planner should take great care in the profile of future and potential creditors. The more sophisticated the creditor the more encumbrances over the assets should be in place.

Transferring any asset falls under the laws and the tax issues of the jurisdictions involved. A fraudulent transfer is a dream come true for a creditor and may give them automatic domain over the asset and the legal right to pursue the transferred assets. This is why we say that the assets should be protected when the seas are calm.

Few of us would hesitate at arranging our affairs to pay less income tax. The majority of people think it moral to try to reduce estate and inheritance taxes. It is legal to reduce taxes without committing fraud or tax evasion. In law, obligation is defined by "duty" and "Duty of Care" means what you owe by specific circumstances.

Then what duty of care does a person owe an injured party? There is a famous saying by lawyers in answering this question, "that depends." Herein is the answer to the question, "Is it ethical to do asset protection planning?"

Should you become the injured party, you will be subject to the ethics of others and will have no control over the outcome or the consequences you will suffer. One could argue that the party who is right will prevail. There are no guarantees and there is no magic wand.

Your solution could be a combination of asset protection trusts, family limited partnerships, insurance, LLCs, or many other various tools in the toolbox. Be aware that the toolbox is filled with many options when the financial seas are calm and that once your assets are financially challenged or in duress, these options become limited.

What Is a Trust?

There are many definitions and different ways to explain what a trust is. Below are a few definitions:

- A trust is the right, enforceable solely in equity, to the beneficial enjoyment of property of which another holds the legal title.
- A trust is a legal relationship in which one person (or qualified trust company) (trustee) holds property for the benefit of another (beneficiary). The property can be any kind of real or personal property-money, real estate, stocks, bonds, collections, business interests, personal possessions, and automobiles. It is often established by one person for the benefit himself or of another.
- A trust is a fictitious legal entity (not a bricks-and-mortar entity) that owns assets for the benefit of a third person (beneficiary).
- It is common to put whole bank and brokerage accounts, as well as homes and other real estate, into a trust.
- A trust is a relationship in which a person, called a grantor, transfers something of value, called an asset, to another person, called a trustee. The trustee then manages and controls this asset for the benefit of a third person, called a beneficiary. An asset is any kind of property.

You will find many definitions in different states or different law books. The above meanings all refer to the same thing.

How Does a Trust Work?

Generally a trust involves at least three people: (1) the grantor (the person who creates the trust, also known as the settler or donor), (2) the trustee (who holds and manages the property for the benefit of the grantor and others), and (3) one or more beneficiaries (who are entitled to the benefits).

The grantor (or settlor) of the trust is the person who set up and gave money to the trust. The trustee of the trust is the person charged with keeping the assets safe, invested properly, and finally distributed to the beneficiary at the proper time. The grantor can decide how the money must be kept (in interest bearing accounts, in real estate, or only in government insured FDIC accounts, etc.), and when it can be distributed. The grantor of the trust can also be the trustee of the trust, if the grantor decides to set the trust up in such a manner (e.g., the grantor sets himself up to be the trustee of a trust for his child).

How Is a Trust Used?

What are the uses of a trust? Trusts have several uses and they can be of much benefit when properly set up and managed. One of the uses of a trust is to provide flexible control of assets for the benefit of minor children. A trust set up for the benefit of minor children can avoid the necessity of further legal proceedings, such as the appointment of a conservator.

A conservator is someone who is appointed by the court to control the assets of minor children. Conservators are restricted by law and must be bonded and file annual accountings with the probate court.

Children cannot legally handle their own financial affairs before they reach the age of 18.

One purpose of creating a trust for a child is to assure the grantor that the child will be benefited but will not have control of the trust assets until the child is older. In establishing a trust, the grantor selects a trustee and specifically instructs the trustee how the assets will be used for the beneficiary.

A trust for the benefit of minors often takes effect when both parents have died. It is usually set up to provide for the support, care, and education of the children until they have reached the age set by their parents to actually receive the assets being held by the trustee.

Putting property in trust transfers it from your personal ownership to the trustee who holds the property for you. The trustee has legal title to the trust property. For most purposes, the law looks at these assets as if they were now owned by the trustee.

For example, many trusts have separate taxpayer identification numbers. But trustees are not the full owners of the property. Trustees have a legal duty to use the property as provided in the trust agreement and as permitted by law. The beneficiaries retain what is known as equitable title, the right to benefit from the property as specified in the trust.

The donor may retain control of the property. Putting assets "in" a trust does not mean that they change location. Think of a trust instead as an imaginary container. It is not a geographical place that protects your car, but a form of ownership that holds it for your benefit. On your car title, the owner blank would simply read "the Mr. Jones Trust."

After your trust comes into being, your assets will probably still be in the same place they were before you set it up—the car in the garage, the money in the bank, the land where it always was—but it will have a different owner: the Mr. Jones Trust, not Mr. Jones.

Offshore Trusts

According to the IRS, in general a trust is a relationship in which one person holds title to property, subject to an obligation to keep or use the property for the benefit of another.

The laws that govern trusts are subject to the jurisdictions in which that trust is recognized whether onshore or offshore. There are domestic trusts called onshore trusts and offshore trusts, which are outside the U.S. domain. It is critical to choose the proper jurisdiction for your trusts because not all jurisdictions offer the same protection and benefits. Some jurisdictions offer favorable protection of assets. (Remember that the beneficiaries enjoy those same assets without holding title.) Other jurisdictions may only offer limited protection.

Most assets, titled and untitled, can be transferred to offshore locations; real estate, cash, stocks, bonds, securities, businesses, precious jewels, gold, and art are examples. The trust company must be knowledgeable and familiar with the statutes and legislation in order that the trustee is afforded the best protection and services available.

The primary benefit of a trust is protection. A judge cannot compel the forfeiture of an asset in a jurisdiction that he does not rule from or from which he has no authority. Therefore, the assets remain safely in place where they have been all along.

Offshore trusts are especially powerful tools of protection because it is unlikely that a creditor would spend the time and money in litigation for the slim chance of gaining anything. A creditor would be forced to begin litigation in the jurisdiction of the trust (if the jurisdiction will even hear the case).

The heart and purpose of trust legislation as set by their statutes is to create a durable entity. It is much like the expression "chasing your tail" and this is not a desirable result for a creditor.

In some jurisdictions you can name yourself as the sole beneficiary, in others you cannot. This is another reason why a plan must be strategically created to fit your individual needs.

It is important that the trustee be bonded and licensed to provide trustee services. In some cases, insurance companies may stand in as the trustee. In any event, the beneficiary may remove the trustee and replace them if they are not satisfied if and only if the provisions have been made in the operating agreement.

Again, this is why an experienced and trusted company should be employed for your asset protection plan because technically the beneficiary owns nothing. If the sound of owning nothing scares you and makes you skeptical, understanding the legal concept of ownership and custody may put you at ease.

A person or entity with custody has full possession and control over a thing regardless of who the owner is. Only the owner can pass this custody and possession, but once it is passed the custodian or possessor (sometimes the same and sometimes not) have the full benefits according to the law. Now you know that placing your property into a trust does not increase your ability to be removed from the benefits of the property or asset.

Often an offshore LLC is used in conjunction with the formation of the trust. This LLC is the management LLC inside the trust and owned 100 percent by the trust. You operate the trust on a day-by-day basis, unless you are in duress, and then by operating agreement policy, the management of the LLC is passed to a licensed and bonded trustee on a temporary basis until the time of legal duress passes.

The trustee to which the trust is passed is outside the jurisdiction of the judgment and therefore does not have to comply with creditors or with the judgment. The assets then remain safely within the trust. This agreement for the trust is set up before any duress occurs, avoiding any fraudulent conveyance.

The time for transfer for avoiding penalties of Fraudulent Conveyance varies in different jurisdictions and by the nature of the asset as well. Some jurisdictions have more favorable movement of assets, but there is one steadfast rule—the assets that are protected with the greatest security are moved before duress, or as we say, when the seas are calm.

Asset Protection FAQs

Question: Why do I need asset protection?

Answer: You need to protect your assets because the dynamics of society are uncontrollable. Regardless of how much money you have, or your position at a company or in government, there are accidents, litigation over disputes, greedy people, terrorism, scams and litigious crazy attorneys. Even if we did not live in an overly litigious society, you would still need asset protection.

Some of the first people to realize that they could be "taken" and needed asset protection were Andrew Carnegie, Henry Ford, and John D. Rockefeller. Incidentally, these great businesspersons realized that they needed asset protection *before* they were millionaires.

Question: Does my risk level determine my need for asset protection?

Answer: No, what determines the need for asset protection is the fact that you have assets. If you value your assets, you need to protect them.

Question: If my assets determine my need, what role does risk play?

Answer: Risk is a determining factor as to what type of protection you may need. There are different ways to protect different assets and different levels of security. This is how a plan works in general.

No longer are professionals and business owners the only high-risk group, now the small businessperson (even the common homeowner) must focus on ways to protect their savings, investments, and other accumulated assets …anyone with anything of value has become attractive targets for greedy and unscrupulous attorneys.

Question: If the legal system is based on justice, then how is it legal and just for me to protect my assets from others?

Answer: The legal system in the United States is stacked against the defendant (the one against whom the suit is brought) and is in favor of the plaintiff. Think about this—a judge must give the claim a "green light" to proceed because the plaintiff has brought sufficient cause and reason in the complaint against the defendant. If the judge feels that the claim has no merit it is dropped. Otherwise the defendant is defending him- or herself against a complaint that a judge has deemed as worthy. This certainly gives the plaintiff an advantage.

Statistics show that even the average person will be sued one to five times in a lifetime and will face the real possibility of being on the losing end of a disastrous judgment. Neglecting to plan for that possibility can result in the instantaneous loss of a lifetime's worth of accumulated assets.

Asset protection is legal by statute (laws). There are several reasons for this based on a history of common law. One reason is that others have rights to your assets or they may benefit from the fruits of your assets, such as your wife, your children, or your employees. The court's role is to protect public interest and the rights of society and not just single individuals. You still have to pay your taxes and conduct your affairs within the limits of the law.

Question: What if I am already in trouble or a lawsuit may be pending?

Answer: Once a suit seems imminent or has been filed, the law frowns on the technology of protecting or moving assets. Note: Although assets may be moved under certain conditions, it is always better to move while the seas are still calm. The time to protect your assets is when the financial seas are calm and you are within your rights to determine who will control, own, and benefit from your estate.

Question: How do lawyers or creditors discover my assets?

Answer: Unless you are protected, this is easy for them. They hire one of many firms that specialize in locating assets. They can locate bank accounts, brokerage accounts, auto, real estate, businesses, and so forth, anything in your name. Most of the time a contingency fee attorney will do an asset search on you before he even bothers to sue you. He wants to make sure you have something of value before he spends his time and money.

There is little about your personal and financial information that cannot be found. However, if the assets are not in your name and are listed in the name of a trustee, finding them becomes much more difficult (if not impossible) and expensive for the plaintiff's lawyer.

Question: How can I prevent someone from taking my assets?

Answer: The best thing you can do is make yourself a smaller target. Using technology, such as insurance, government plans, estate planning vehicles and other specifically designed entities, you will effectively shrink the size of your estate in the eyes of the creditor. You still control and benefit from your assets. As John D. Rockefeller said, "Own nothing and control everything." That is the key. You do not ever need to give up control, but you can give up ownership in such a way that a plaintiff will give up and look for greener pastures.

This is done through a combination of domestic and foreign structures.

Question: Are these techniques legal?

Answer: Absolutely, the rich have practiced asset protection for decades. They use these tools and strategies that we are discussing. They are legal, effective, and can give you the peace of mind you have earned. The Center for Financial, Legal, and Tax Planning, Inc., has perfected a process that makes proper asset protection affordable to people.

Question: Who puts this plan in place—attorneys, insurance brokers, financial planners, estate and trust planners? I am not sure who to hire.

Answer: The answer is a combination of the above. It requires specific knowledge in each area of protection. Your attorney will consult when necessary. Asset protection is not taught as part of the training in law school; it is a specialized area. Consequently, if an attorney is not careful he or she can lose their license if it appears that they assisted a client in hiding assets. For that reason, the number of attorneys skilled in asset protection is limited. If your particular situation warrants it, we will direct you to qualified attorneys who can help you once you have made the decision to protect.

Summary

Asset protection is not for everybody—only for those individuals with assets! A comprehensive plan is necessarily unique to an individual and their particular circumstances. Planning must, that is, *must* be undertaken well in advance of any litigation in order to avoid "fraudulent transfer" issues. Through a combination of trusts (domestic and/or offshore) and other legal entities, a high net-worth individual can retain control of their assets while fully immunizing them from potential creditors. Consultation with a knowledgeable planner is expressly advised.

Profound Insight #6

All the world is a stage and most of us are unrehearsed.

CHAPTER 7

Shifting the Risk Equation— Insurance Maneuvers

Boxing is a rather amorphous body, though recognizable because it is headless.

—*Bob Verdi*

Key Employee Insurance

Many business owners may understand the merits of having their business own a life insurance policy on a key employee. But also like many business owners, they may not be aware of new requirements on such insurance imposed by recent legislation. Let us explore the concept of key employee insurance and then review the new requirements.

Even though key assets in a business include things such as its plant, equipment, inventory, and accounts receivable, the utilization of these assets by its key people is the main reason why a business enjoys success.

These key assets are replaceable—they may be insured against loss due to fire, theft, the weather, and other hazards. And although the loss caused by these events may significantly disrupt the business, the loss is usually temporary. In fact, after a fire loss, the replaced or repaired plant often turns out to be better than the original. Additionally, the probability of a loss by fire is many times less than the loss caused by the death of a key employee. The loss due to the death of a key person is permanent, even though someone else may eventually fill the position.

Receiving cash, free of taxation, is one of the best things that can happen to a business that is suffering from the death of a key employee. For example, let us say the business was nearing the final stages on a bid for some new business when the project manager died from a motorcycle accident. There probably were expenses incurred in developing the bid that will never be recovered unless the bid is accepted and the project completed. The customer, other employees, and the business's creditors are likely to be quite concerned. An infusion of cash at this time will not complete the bid but will surely quiet the concerns until someone else can complete the bid and follow through if the contract is awarded.

Life insurance on a key employee has saved many firms from the junk heap because, at the death of the key employee, cash was provided at the precise time it was needed the most. This impact of cash infusion does not only benefit the business and business owner—the employees and their families benefit from the cash provided by the life insurance.

Although the concept of key employee insurance is easy to understand, the process for securing the insurance is a bit more complicated.

In the case of employer-owned life insurance, according to the Internal Revenue Service, "the amount excluded from gross income of an applicable policyholder" under Section 101(a)(1) of the Internal Revenue Code, "shall not exceed an amount equal to the sum of the premiums and other amounts paid by the policyholder for the contract." Thus, all the proceeds from a policy owned by an employer are to be included in income, subject to several exceptions.

Section 101(j) of the Internal Revenue Code, added by the Pension Protection Act of 2006, except for:

Policies for which the insured is an employee at any time during the 12-month period before the insured's death, when the policy is legitimately used for:

Key employees (directors or highly compensated individuals under Section 414(q) or Section 105(h)(5), (the top 35 percent rather than 25 percent); Life insurance as an employee benefit (financing deferred compensation arrangements, or postretirement health insurance); income exclusion for these uses is secured when the beneficiaries are family members of the insured, the designated beneficiary, other than the employer, a trust established for the benefit of any such person, or the estate of the insured;

Buy-sell arrangements, where the policy amount is used to purchase "an equity (or capital or profits) interest in the applicable policyholder from any person described" in the above exceptions.

Once the exceptions have been identified and met, there is still another step to make sure that the life insurance proceeds are not included in taxable income. The notice and consent requirements must be met.

The insured must be notified that his or her employer intends to insure their life and that the employer will benefit from their death by being the beneficiary along with the amount of coverage.

The employee must consent in writing to the insurance and that the insurance continues even after terminating employment.

It sounds complicated, but do not let these requirements deter you from carefully considering this type of life insurance—a qualified insurance representative can help you wade through the regulations. The survival of a business depends on making sound business decisions, including the decision to insure key employees.

LTCi for the Business Owner

Many of us have heard statistics about what percentage of people will enter a nursing home after age 65—it is a substantial number. But forget the statistics and bring the thought of nursing home care down to a personal level: consider how a long-term care event would affect your family and your business. For small business owners, long-term care insurance (LTCi) is not about picking your nursing home or whether to receive care at home or in a facility, it is about asset protection.

Certainly you have considered the fate of your business once you reach retirement age. Some of you may dream of cashing out and retiring. Others, especially people who want to keep a business in the family, may consider easing into a part-time retirement. Whatever the dream, the reality is that many business owners will not be given the choice and will require long-term care before their intended retirement date.

What happens if you need services while you still own the business? Could your business afford to pay you your income, your replacement's salary, and pay for your additional care expenses? Businesses that do not manage expenses cannot survive and thrive.

The good news is that you can obtain long-term care insurance and shift this risk to an insurance company. By lengthening the exclusion period or using riders correctly like shared-care benefits, you can manage the cost. Also, the shared-care benefits riders allow you to borrow from your spouse's benefit pool. However, it is important to obtain a knowledgeable insurance agent.

If you do purchase long-term care insurance, be certain that you are taking advantage of all tax benefits available to you. Since 1997 the government has provided tax benefits to those who purchase these contracts—especially business owners.

If your business is organized as a sole proprietorship, S corporation, LLC, or partnership, and you have net income from self-employment, you are eligible to deduct certain eligible premium amounts paid by the business for you, your spouse, and your tax dependents. These eligible premiums are published and indexed for inflation every year.

The insurance plan must be established by your business, but you are not required to provide the benefit to all of your employees. If you do pay for your employees' policies though, the premiums are deductible without regard to the eligible premium limitations discussed above.

If your business is taxed as a C (regular) corporation, the benefits are even greater. You can still deduct the premiums paid for you, your spouse, and your tax dependents, but now you are not limited to the eligible premium amounts.

Benefits paid under a qualified long-term care insurance contract are generally tax-free as well. If you purchase a contract that only reimburses you for actual long-term care expenses incurred, no tax will be owed. If you purchase a policy that pays you a cash benefit regardless of the cost of care, benefits paid in excess of the actual costs or a "per diem" amount (also published and indexed for inflation annually) will be considered taxable income. See Exhibit 7.1.

An appropriate risk analysis for your assets must take into account the possibility of asset depletion due to the need for long-term care services. Is it worthwhile? It may just help your business survive to the next generation.

Exhibit 7.1 LTCi premiums Tax status

Type of Business	Who Pays Premium	Deductibility
Sole Proprietor	Employer pays premiums for employee's policies.	Employer deducts 100% of premium expense. Premiums paid by employer are not included in employee's taxable income. Benefits from policy are not included in recipients, taxable income.
	Sole proprietor pays premiums for own policy.	Deducts lesser of actual premiums paid or eligible long-term care insurance premium. Benefits received from policy not included in taxable income.
Partnership	Employer pays premiums for employee's policies.	Employer deducts 100% of premium expense. Premiums paid by employer are not included in employee's taxable income. Benefits from policy are not included in recipients' taxable income.
	Partnership pays premiums for partner's policy.	Premiums attributed to each partner included in their income. Partner deducts lesser of actual premiums paid or eligible long-term care insurance premium. Benefits received from policy not included in taxable income.
C Corporation (Includes 501 (c)(3) charities)	Employer pays premiums for employee's policies.	Employer deducts 100% of premium expense. Premiums paid by employer are not included in employee's taxable income. Benefits from policy are not included in recipients' taxable income.

Entity	Action	Tax Treatment
S Corporation	Employer pays premiums for employees' policies (including 2% or less shareholders).	Employer deducts 100% of premium expense. Premiums paid by employer are not included in employee's taxable income. Benefits from policy are not included in recipients' taxable income.
	S Corporation pays premiums for greater than 2% shareholders policies.	Premiums attributed to each shareholder included in their income. Shareholder deducts lesser of actual premiums paid or eligible long-term care insurance premium. Benefits received from policy not included in taxable income.
LLC (taxed as a partnership)	Employer pays premiums for employees' policies.	Employer deducts 100% of premium expense. Premiums paid by employer are not included in employee's taxable income. Benefits from policy are not included in recipients' taxable income.
	LLC pays premiums for owner/members' policies.	Premiums attributed to each owner/member included in their income. Owner/member deducts lesser of actual premiums paid or eligible long-term care insurance premium. Benefits received from policy not included in taxable income.

Source: IRC Sec. 162(I)(I)(B), Rev. Rul. 91–26, 1991–15 I.R.B. 23.

Life Insurance for Business Continuation

Like many other business owners, you may not be interested, at least initially, in looking at how you can keep your business going if something happens to you. Certainly, your first priority is to make your business profitable and successful—how to keep your business thriving when you are no longer in the picture can be dealt with later. Postponing that dilemma could be a mistake, however.

A business continuation agreement, which could be a solution, may be down on your priority list for many reasons: it might be too expensive, there may not be a qualified buyer of the business, or you just may be unsure about your future plans. However, there is one thing that you undoubtedly are sure of—you want to use your business to take care of your family and a life insurance policy will help you do this.

A life insurance policy on a business owner's life secures the business, the employees, and the business owner's own family.

For example, if the value of your business is $500,000, you could purchase a $500,000 life insurance policy, payable to your family as beneficiary. You (or your spouse) could also be the owner of the policy. Because the policy is owned outside of the business, it may be outside of the claims of the creditors of the business (some state statutes may also exempt life insurance from the claims of any creditor). If something happens to you, your family is taken care of regardless of what happens to your business. Your family has the time to find a buyer for the business, continue the business on their own, or your family could even liquidate the business, if desired.

This idea might have some appeal for the following reasons:

- It is simple to understand.
- Any type of life insurance product (term, universal life, etc.) can be used.

- It does not depend on any tax rules or regulations.
- It does not prevent 'the use of a business continuation agreement in the future.
- This is a plan that you, as the business owner, can implement *today*.

It's a simple solution worth considering.

Summary

There are a multitude of risk-shifting insurance products that provide unique solutions to the myriad problems associated with business ownership. Complexities in the tax code mandate the use of an insurance advisor well-versed in the peculiarities of business-owned insurance policies. Planning for the ongoing success of the business, as well as ensuring the financial stability of the business owner and their family is, and will remain, one of the primary considerations of any business owner. Insurance products such as Key Person and LTCi address some of those needs particularly well.

Profound Insight #7

Anything that doesn't eat you today is saving you for tomorrow.

CHAPTER 8

Reevaluating Existing Insurance

The bell that tolls for all in boxing belongs to a cash register.

—*Bob Verdi*

I s your life insurance supposed to be paid up by now, but is not? Notices from insurance companies may even indicate that their suggested premium payment has increased, or that your policies are about to lapse.

Is your "investment type" life insurance policy not performing as projected? Ever cancel your life insurance and get a taxable statement of gain? This can even happen if your policy lapses and you get nothing back (a so-called "paper gain"). This is becoming more common.

Evaluation or Audit

There are many reasons why it can be advantageous for the owner of a cash value life insurance policy to exchange an old policy for a newer one.

These reasons include:

- Reducing premium payments substantially
- The insured's improved health
- A change in the rating of the insurance company
- Competitive terms of a new policy

- Increasing the death benefit while making the same payment
- Increase in the endowment age for the insured
- Change in the insured's financial situation

and many more.

When interest rates dropped, premiums had to be paid, in some cases, for twice as long. Instead of cashing in a value life insurance policy and purchasing a new one, a policy owner can use an insurance audit or evaluator process on the policies.

By doing so, a policy owner can roll the existing cash value insurance policy into a new one without paying taxes on the growth in the old policy's cash value. In contrast, if the policy owner were to cancel the policy, she would be subject to paying income tax on the cash value in excess of premiums paid into the policy.

An insurance exchange also allows the policy owner to carry over the original basis, which is used to calculate income taxes due upon receiving distributions from the policy's cash value. Maintaining the original basis can be especially beneficial in the initial contract years of the policy, when the premiums paid may exceed the policy's cash value.

As an example, a life insurance policy on which the owner has paid $30,000 in premiums has a cash value of $20,000. If the owner were to surrender the policy and buy a new one with the proceeds, the basis in the new policy would be $20,000. Using a 1035 exchange, however, the basis would remain at $30,000.

Because people are living longer, and due to the insurance marketplace having become more efficient and competitive, the cost of death protection on new policies is usually lower than on older policies.

Clients with old policies that don't reflect updated mortality experience may benefit by swapping them for policies with lower premiums or higher death benefits. One problem with older policies is that they were illustrated at high interest rates that probably would not last indefinitely. These policies might have illustrated being paid up in, say, 11 years, and when interest rates dropped, premiums had to be paid for, in some cases, twice as long.

The insurance audit process takes advantage of the tax regulations that allow taxes gained to be deferred or eliminated on the gain within a policy as long as the proceeds are used to buy a "similar" policy. Similar means the same owner, insured, and beneficiary.

Thus, a life insurance audit allows us to essentially trade a bad policy for a better one. Bad policies include those of the variable sort that have underperformed market expectations, or those issued before the current life tables that now grant more favorable premiums.

For example, typically new mortality tables are established every decade, which have historically granted longer life expectancies to the population. It is axiomatic that it will be cheaper to insure a person today on the new mortality tables. There is an expectation that they could live to a maximum of age 120, versus a person on the older mortality table where it was expected a person would live to a maximum of age 100.

Further, advances in software modeling and increased efficiency (and competition) in the market have allowed (or forced) carriers to underwrite more modern policies with less "fat" than older ones. Thus again, the policies increase benefits for the consumer.

It is incumbent on the practitioner to ask about the existing policies of clients, whether sold by them or not. A CPA with an insurance license is not merely able to sell insurance—that CPA will be held accountable (pun intended) and held to a higher standard regarding insurance policies than a CPA without a license.

That license may well become a liability. The practitioner *must* review policies—whether by himself or by bringing in an experienced life insurance agent who will then be able to "shop" carriers for more efficient policies. A policy exchange is not necessarily appropriate for every client or every policy—care must be taken to avoid abuse. However, a life insurance audit is most definitely appropriate for every client, especially those carrying older policies, which are more likely to be improved. Only when the client's best interest is served should an exchange be performed.

Efficiency can bring lower premiums for the same (or better) death benefit, or perhaps take existing cash value and eliminate the need for future premiums. If the actual underlying need for the insurance no longer exists, such as insurance used to protect a mortgage, which has since been paid off, and the client no longer even wants the coverage, one option is to dump the policy in favor of the existing cash value. Most large, reputable insurance companies allow this option.

The industry is highly regulated, and many carriers still have black eyes from dubious practices in the recent past regarding cash values. Thus, they are extremely conservative. However, simply offering an insured the cash value of his policy may NOT be the sole option available to that consumer, and may in fact leave the advisor open to malpractice claims.

According to Mark Boehm, MBA, CWPP™, an industry expert who specializes in improving older policies:

The vast majority of the policies in force today are not meeting the clients' original objectives. Many were poorly designed in relation to premium deposit strategy, have high costs with low probability of success, and will 'implode' or lapse at an age that is much younger than previously illustrated. Virtually all have not been annually monitored since issue, and may contractually increase the premium, which the client will not be prepared for or understand. A properly performed audit will yield significant improvements to a substantial majority of all the life insurance currently in-force.

This is the result of an industry that has not trained agents in the understanding of new paradigm (universal life and variable universal life) structure. Similar problems exist with these policies that have secondary guarantees, as well as policies with heavy term blends and participating whole life.

I see a questionable level of professionalism in the methodology, design, and application of life insurance policies by planners. To be fair, I also come across planning strategies and product integration that was well designed, communicated, and implemented. But that is not the norm.

Instead, accept the fact that there is an almost 83 percent probability that life and annuity policies owned by [you] are in trouble. Embrace the fact that almost 83 percent of the proposals that [you] will be exposed to will become problematic.

Make a decision—Will you be passive or active in this arena? If passive, understand that what you have, or will buy, may not be advantageous for you. If active, perform an inventory analysis. You should consult with your tax professional before purchasing anything.

Consultative Leverage

Most of the regulatory bodies are getting more concerned and sensitive about policy replacement, but replacements are still taking place with great frequency. In many cases, the initiative is to produce commission, as the summary analysis provided lacks depth and usually misses the factual issues. This is the transactional approach.

The problem for the client is that you are transferring assets (cash value) from an existing policy to that which may not be more cost-efficient, but more importantly, introduces you into a new period of surrender charges and illiquidity.

When challenged, the agent–planner who proposed the replacement will be hard-pressed to quantify the true economical benefits for the change and to justify any reasoning for the new commission and new surrender charges.

As an example: A 50-year-old male, preferred nonsmoker, has a $1 million policy with $180,000 of cash surrender value. When an illustration is used to demonstrate the policy's potential, it can make this policy appear an excellent choice. A chart for the policy having an assumed 6.5 percent interest rate makes the policy look a good choice, but the actual current interest rate was the minimum guaranteed rate of 4 percent.

The high interest rate assumption initially used helped to cover up a costly policy.

With a well-designed policy, the first year guaranteed cash value can be in excess of the amount transferred ($181,332 cash value on the $180,000 1035 transfer). This really comes home to roost if you look at a comparison with most typical policies.

A sidebar to this case is that the example policy is a continuous premium, which did not carry the policy as long as the new policy with only the 1035 funds. This difference would allow the client to save on an expense and he was free to fly around the country (or more seriously, invest in those policies no longer requiring premiums).

An insurance exchange is the most efficient way to accomplish various fundamental insurance planning goals. Don't attempt this on your own, and be wary of your local insurance agent who may say he can help. The result may be a large tax bill.

Under Internal Revenue Code Section 1035, insurance can be exchanged for insurance or annuities. However, because such exchanges are complicated, many mistakes can be made. Any mistake can make the exchange useless or, worse, taxable (in a gain situation). There is also a liability issue.

Section 1035 does not require state insurance department replacement forms to be filed. But the filing and analysis of state insurance department replacement forms are part of the insurance exchange procedure. So is the analysis of new acquisition costs, cancellation penalties, new contestability periods, and so forth. Exchanges should only be recommended if advantages outweigh the disadvantages.

Aaron Skloff, Accredited Investment Fiduciary (AIF), Chartered Financial Analyst (CFA), Master of Business Administration (MBA), CEO of Skloff Financial Group a registered investment advisory firm, and insurance expert, comments on 1035 exchanges: "The insurance industry is littered with insurance salespeople who have no interest in how a 1035 will benefit the client…they simply want to make a buck." He further highlights in an article entitled "Is Your Life Insurance Eroding?" that an insurance policy owner considering a 1035 exchange "…work with a licensed insurance agent that has in-depth analytical skills."

Summary

Many existing insurance policies are underperforming and in potential danger of lapsing. A thorough evaluation of existing policies should be performed by competent advisors using a consultative process. Be wary of insurance salespeople trying to sell you a "new and improved" policy—make sure the benefits to the client are demonstrably well documented.

Profound Insight #8

Before you give a colleague a piece of your mind, be sure you can spare it.

CHAPTER 9

What Financial Advisors "Forget" to Tell Their Clients

A boxer never sees the big one that hits him.

—George Foreman

D o you ever get the feeling that financial advisors are looking out for themselves instead of their clients? You may be right. In most cases they are looking out for themselves.

Unfortunately, many financial advisors ("brokers") do not have an accounting or finance degree. They have simply passed securities or insurance exams and the state and the federal authorities unleash them on the public. Even if they want to act in their client's best interest many times they do not have the skill set to do so.

To make matters worse, in most instances the financial advisor has a relatively light level of responsibility called *suitability*. The suitability rules require that when a broker recommends that a client buy or sell a particular security, the broker must have a reasonable basis for believing that the recommendation is suitable for that client. In making this assessment, your broker must consider the client's risk tolerance, other security holdings, financial situation (income and net worth), financial needs, and investment objectives.[1]

Suitability abuse can be broadly defined as recommending or implementing an inappropriate investment based on a client's age or risk level, failing to disclose risks associated with an investment or failing to disclose materially important information that may lead to a more informed decision.

Let us look at an example of suitability abuse. A financial advisor calls Mr. X and says they should buy an S&P 500 stock index mutual fund, as it is a suitable investment. Mr. X agrees and asks for a recommendation. If the financial advisor recommends the high load, high expense S&P 500 index mutual fund managed by the same firm the financial advisor works for instead of a no-load, low expense S&P 500 index mutual fund from another company, the financial advisor *has* met the suitability requirement. Coincidentally, the financial advisor would also receive a higher level of compensation.

How can that be, you ask? Because the cards are stacked against the client. Clearly, suitability is not concerned about the best or most favorable service or product.

To make matters even worse, many financial advisors work for publicly traded financial service companies. You know the ones that have their names on baseball stadiums, advertise during the Super Bowl, and have their names stitched on the shirts of professional golfers.

These publicly traded companies do not remain in existence for the good of clients. They remain in existence for the good of shareholders. Can you imagine the chairman or chief executive officer (CEO) of one of those publicly traded companies coming on the evening news broadcast to say they place their clients' interest before their shareholders? First off, they will have violated the law. All publicly traded companies must act in the best interest of shareholders, *not* clients. Second off, their head would be on the chopping block.

No shareholder in their right mind would allow the chairman or any other board member to place any other party's interest ahead of their own. The shareholders hired the board to make sure management runs the company in the best interest of the owners—the shareholders, *not* clients.

If you do not see a problem here—stop reading and keep putting more money in the "financial advisor's" pocket. If you see a problem here—keep reading for the simple solution.

Fiduciary Duty

Fiduciary duty—two simple words, yet oh so powerful. Many different types of professionals owe a fiduciary duty to someone—for example, lawyers to their clients, trustees to their beneficiaries, and corporate officers to their shareholders.[2] Critically Important: The U.S. Supreme Court has determined that financial advisors registered under the Investment Advisers Act of 1940 ("Act") are fiduciaries. The word fiduciary comes from the Latin word for "trust." A fiduciary must act for the benefit of the person to whom he owes fiduciary duties, to the exclusion of any contrary interest.

Many financial services companies intentionally avoid registering their financial advisors under the Act for one simple reason—to avoid fiduciary duty.

That is right—they do *not* want to be obligated by law to act in the best interest of clients. Let us go back to the example of the financial advisor who recommended the higher cost, higher commission mutual fund. If the financial advisor were registered under the Act the financial advisor would be obligated to act in the best interest of the client and would be obligated to recommend the lower cost solution.

Interestingly, the financial advisor would be prohibited by law to accept a commission. That is right. A financial advisor registered under the Act is legally called an Investment Advisor Representative (IAR) and must work for a company legally called a Registered Investment Advisor (RIA). Neither an IAR nor an RIA is permitted to be compensated by commission. Rather, both can be compensated only by fees.

Imagine lying on the operating room table as your neurological surgeon is evaluating which scalpel to use on your left frontal lobe of your brain for your procedure. Scalpel one is made by a company that pays him a higher commission than the company that made scalpel two. Preposterous? Not in the context of how many financial advisors "operate."

An RIA and the firm's IARs are obligated by law to act in the best interest of clients and are compensated with fees—just like a neurological surgeon. Many fee arrangements are tied to the value of assets being managed. This creates an equitable relationship with you and your IAR. If your assets increase in value your fees increase, as your assets decrease in value your fees decrease. It sounds fair because it is.

So, how do less reputable firms get around this "problem"? They register as an RIA, yet are very careful to register the RIA business as *ancillary* to their overall business. If the RIA business is ancillary to their overall business (which may include investment banking, broker dealer, merchant bank, banking, and so forth), then they can mitigate their fiduciary duty.

Which brings us to a simple solution to all these conflicts and qualifications, like Mom used to say, "Get it in writing!" If you want the investment firm you are dealing with to place your client's interests above and beyond their interests, have them clearly accept fiduciary duty in writing on their company letterhead.

Don't be surprised if your financial advisor says "that's not necessary," or "that's essentially what it says on page 1,847 of the contract you signed," or "our compliance department prohibits that."

Protect yourself. Have the firm give you a simple letter

Exhibit 9.1   Example Fiduciary Statement

Skloff Financial Group

Acceptance of Fiduciary Duty

Skloff Financial Group, a Registered Investment Advisor (RIA), accepts fiduciary duty for all financial planning and investment management services provided to Jane Smith. Skloff Financial Group will place Jane Smith's interests before Aaron Skloff, any employee of the company, shareholder of the company or any other party.

Aaron Skloff

Aaron Skloff, AIF, CFA, MBA

CEO—Skloff Financial Group

signed by a principal of the company, like the one shown in Exhibit 9.1.

Summary

The selection and utilization of a financial advisor is as important as the selection and utilization of a surgeon. You should understand their academic background, credentials, and experience. Unfortunately, your due diligence does not end there. As discussed in this chapter, you must understand whether your financial advisor will accept fiduciary duty in writing, on company letterhead. Lastly, understand what conflicts of interest that acceptance may have if the financial advisor's employer is a public company—obligated by law to place shareholders' interests above your own. Remember, it's your wealth—not their wealth.

Profound Insight #9

Q: Why is a stockbroker's advice so cheap?

A: Because supply always exceeds demand.

Notes

1. Broker-Dealers: "Why They Ask for Personal Information," modified 03/26/08, www.sec.gov/answers/bd-persinfo.htm.
2. Lori A. Richards, Director, Office of Compliance Inspections and Examinations U.S. Securities and Exchange Commission, Eighth Annual Investment Adviser Compliance Summit, Washington, DC, 02/27/06, www.sec.gov/news/speech/spch022706lar.htm.

CHAPTER 10

The Truth About
Variable Annuities

Boxing has become America's tragic theater.

—*Joyce Carol Oates*

Have you ever wondered why so many of your clients own variable annuities (VA)? On review of these variable annuities, do you frequently see the word "guarantee"? Guarantee, what does that mean these days? Let us explore the answer to this question as we gain an understanding of variable annuities.

The typical VA acts as a tax-deferred tax shelter, like a Traditional IRA or 401(k). Unlike a Traditional IRA or 401(k), a client can open any size (e.g., $1,000 or $1 million) VA, independent of their income, age, or employment status. This is quite attractive for clients looking to shelter income from taxation, particularly for those who cannot achieve their goal with a Traditional IRA or 401(k).

As a reminder, Traditional IRAs can only be established by persons under the age of 70½ and those (or the spouse of those, if married filing jointly) who receive income or alimony. With a 401(k), your client must be employed to be eligible to make contributions. Each vehicle has contribution limits, which limit the tax-sheltering benefits.

In almost all cases a variable annuity is a form of life insurance. The typical financial planner (translation: insurance salesperson), markets the variable annuity as a way to safely invest in the financial markets without risking your client's principal. We all know there is no such thing as a free lunch inside or outside the world of finance.

The insurance salesperson will often tell your client you cannot earn less than 6 or 7 percent on the investment. This is only part of the story, and—as you have probably already imagined—only the good part.

Variable Annuity Components

Inherent in most VA policies are two components: (1) an investment component, and (2) an insurance component. The investment component offers a choice of investments similar to mutual funds, called subaccounts. It is the insurance component that takes a bit of time to understand.

In its simplest form, the insurance component of a VA includes a death benefit. The death benefit "guarantees" (see section entitled: Guarantees) the beneficiary will receive the greater of:

- Value of the VA at death
- The total of all contributions

Let's look at an example of an investor, whose portfolio was *100 percent* invested in a stock subaccount. Assuming the investor invested $5,000 each year for 20 years, contributions would total $100,000. If the average net return per year were 7 percent, the VA would be worth approximately $205,000 at the end of 20 years.

One day this same investor turns on the evening news to learn the stock market has declined *50 percent* in one day. (Note: the worst annual return of the S&P 500 index was −43.34 percent in 1931.) The investor quickly does some calculations in his head, realizes his VA is worth $102,500, has a heart attack, and dies on the spot. His beneficiary would receive the greater of $102,500 or $100,000. In this case the beneficiary would receive $102,500.

So, where was the death benefit? There was *no* death benefit. The only time the beneficiary receives a death benefit is when the policy value falls below the total value of contributions made *and* the investor dies.

Mortality and Expense Charges

Well, at least the investor did not have to pay any expenses for a death benefit they did not receive, right? Wrong. Inherent in the vast majority of VA policies are mortality and expense charges, called M&E charges. The "E," or expense charge, represents the administrative component of the M&E. The "M," or mortality charge, represents the life insurance component of M&E. Unlike traditional life insurance, where the insurance company conducts an extensive review of your medical history and fluid samples, your health is irrelevant with a VA policy. How can that be?

Economics would dictate that the insurance company earns a large enough profit on M&E charges that they can simply insure everyone, including the ill. Fortunately, for the insurance company, stock markets generally provide positive results over the vast majority of their policy holders' lives.

According to Morningstar Inc., as of December 31, 2008, the industry average annual annuity charge for nongroup open-variable annuity contracts was 1.37 percent. But, that is not where the costs end. In addition to M&E charges, most VA policies have surrender costs. These are penalties assessed on the policy if the investor moves the policy before the surrender period ends. Some insurance companies offer annuities with 10 to 12 surrender periods and 12 to 15 percent surrender charges—something has to pay for the "financial advisor's" commission. Of course, this is in addition to all underlying costs of the subaccounts (similar to expense ratios inside all mutual funds).

Fortunately, there is an alternative to high cost, high surrender penalty VA policies. A handful of companies offer no-load, low cost, no surrender penalty VA policies. An investor can transfer for one annuity to another annuity without tax consequences, like an IRA transfer, but it must be handled with care.

Like an IRA transfer, the transfer of a VA policy should be conducted on a custodian to custodian basis. The transfer qualifies as a tax-free transfer if conducted using Internal Revenue Code 1035. A "1035 Exchange," as it is commonly called, is the transfer of one insurance policy into another insurance policy. Handled incorrectly, and the investor could have a taxable distribution and hefty tax bill to boot.

Guarantees

During weak financial market periods, such as the recent period from October 2007 through March 2009, insurance companies have been quick to highlight the "guarantee" in their VA policies. A word of caution on that "guarantee": it is not a guarantee by the U.S. federal government. Unlike FDIC, the guarantee provided by an insurance company is a promise by a company (like a promise by now-bankrupt Enron) supported by a reserve fund that each insurance company must contribute toward in each state it conducts business. For many states the limit is $100,000 per person, per insurance company.

Summary

Variable annuities are powerful tax shelters. When stripped down to their core benefit, tax sheltering, they can be an appropriate vehicle if you are interested in sheltering income and taxes. Unfortunately, the insurance companies that issue these products allow greed to get in the way of offering a tax shelter. By the time they have added all their bells and whistles, you have an overpriced life insurance policy. Fortunately, a handful of insurance companies now offer low-priced variable annuities without all the expensive bells and whistles.

Always read the fine print of your variable annuity contract or hire an experienced professional to assist you before entering into a variable annuity contract—ideally a fiduciary who will accept fiduciary duty in writing on company letterhead.

Profound Insight #10

John Smith was a rich old man dying from natural causes after a long and fruitful life. On his deathbed, he called for his insurance agent, doctor, and preacher:

"I trusted each of you my entire life. Now I want to give each of you $25,000 cash in an envelope to put in my grave. I want to take it with me."

Mr. Smith died and at the funeral, each one placed the envelope on top of the man, then he was laid to rest.

On the way back from the funeral, in the limo, the doctor confessed "I must tell you gentlemen, I only put $10,000 on top of our old friend John. I wanted to buy this new machine that would enable me to better care for my patients. It's what he would have wanted."

Then the preacher said: "I have to confess, I only put $5,000 in the coffin. We needed that money to help more homeless, and it's what John would've wanted."

The insurance agent was angry at both the men, and said: "I can't believe the two of you, stealing from a dead man. I wrote a check for the full $25,000!"

CHAPTER 11

What Life Insurance Agents "Forget" to Tell Their Clients

I only have to read Joe Louis' name and my nose starts to bleed again.
—Tommy Fair

Have you ever wondered why an insurance agent is more concerned about gaining entry into the Million Dollar Round Table (MDRT) than he or she is with providing your client the best insurance solution? When is the last time an insurance agent concluded that your client had too much insurance? Unfortunately, many insurance agents are more concerned about themselves than they are with their clients.

Questionable Aspirations

The insurance industry is littered with groups and associations that pride themselves on meeting sales goals. Please do not get me wrong, an honest and reputable insurance agent may generate enough business to receive industry recognition and claim. In fact, commerce is the blood that flows through the veins of the tremendous and successful U.S. economy. But, meeting a sales goal does not provide the client any benefit. To the contrary, it may perpetuate unethical sales practices and inappropriate insurance solutions.

The Million Round Table (MDRT), the Premier Association of Financial Professionals, calls itself "an international, independent association of more than 31,000 members, or less than 1 percent, of the world's most successful life insurance and financial services professionals from 476 companies in 80 nations and territories." Success can be measured in a multitude of ways. Like many of its brethren in the industry, MDRT's primary measure of success is the amount of premium its members have sold to their clients.

Many insurance agents strive for admittance into associations like MDRT because their employers may give them an extra bonus or because it makes them a more attractive candidate to a prospective employer with similar values. Some agents may simply feed their own egos with what they earn, regardless of how it helps or hurts their clients. High sales volumes may be an outcome to delivering the most appropriate solutions—they should not be a primary driver to strive toward.

Coverage Needs

Many insurance agents would suggest that the right amount of coverage is the maximum you can afford to pay. The more insurance you purchase, the higher the agent's commission. Although that may coincidentally be the right amount of coverage, it may considerably more than is necessary.

The ideal way to determine the correct amount of coverage is to complete a needs analysis, as seen in Exhibit 11.1.

Estate Taxes

Death and taxes are unavoidable…or are they? Unfortunately, there are no solutions to avoid death. Taxes on the other hand are avoidable. One of the most devastating taxes is the U.S. deferral estate tax. Without estate tax planning, assets are

Exhibit 11.1   Needs Analysis Worksheet Example

Add		
Spouse's Annual Expenses	20 Years × $30,000	$600,000
Children's Annual Expenses	20 Years × $20,000	$400,000
Child 1 College Expenses	4 Years × $20,000	$80,000
Child 2 College Expenses	4 Years × $25,000	$100,000
Subtotal		$1,180,000
Subtract		
Savings		$50,000
Employer Life Insurance	1 × $130,000 Salary	$130,000
Subtotal		$180,000
Total Insurance Needed		**$1,000,000**

subject to U.S. federal estate taxes. There is an unlimited exemption when assets pass to your spouse. Spouses who inherit the estate of the deceased are really just delaying the estate tax. In fact, they may be creating an even greater estate tax liability.

Listed in Exhibit 11.2 are the U.S. federal estate tax and the applicable exemptions.

Those numbers are not a misprint. You will pay these outrageous rates without proper estate planning. You may be thinking, "I don't have $3,500,000 today and probably won't have $1,000,000 in 2011." If you add up all your assets, you

Exhibit 11.2   U.S. Federal Estate Tax Exemptions and Rates

Year	Exemption	Tax Rate
2009	$3,500,000	45%
2010	Estate Tax Repealed	0%
2011	$1,000,000	55%

Exhibit 11.3   Estate

Assets	
Life Insurance Proceeds	$1,000,000
Primary Residence	600,000
401(k) Plan	300,000
IRAs	200,000
Car	30,000
Total	**$2,130,000**

may just exceed both numbers. And, do not forget that many states have their own state estate tax on top of the federal estate tax. For example, the state of New Jersey has a mere $750,000 exemption per person and maximum state estate tax rate of 16 percent per person.

See an example of an estate in Exhibit 11.3.

That's right, life insurance is an asset in your client's estate. Your beneficiary does not pay taxes on the proceeds from your life insurance policy, but it is included in your estate. Without proper estate planning the majority of your client's estate may be subject to estate taxes (to the tune of a combined 70 percent).

The ILIT

Fortunately, life insurance does not need to be part of your estate. With an Irrevocable Life Insurance Trust (ILIT) you can protect one of your largest assets, the proceeds from your life insurance policy, from both federal and state estate taxes. Sorry tax collectors—those are the rules.

Rather than paying unnecessary estate taxes, you can work with an estate planning attorney to establish an ILIT. After a trust is established, your client can name a trustee other than the client to purchase a life insurance policy on your life. The client then gifts the price of the policy to the trust. The clients stipulate who the beneficiaries are on the policy, how the beneficiaries will receive the proceeds, and what conditions must be met to receive the proceeds.

The trust is exempt from estate taxes, the proceeds from the life insurance policy are not part of your client's estate and are not taxable to their beneficiaries. Sorry tax collectors—those are the rules.

Summary

Insurance agents focused on placing their own best interest before your best interest may recommend the wrong type or wrong amount of insurance. Conduct your own research or utilize an agent who measures success with the quality of solutions and education they provide—not the amount of insurance they sell.

Profound Insight #11

A drunk wanders into the lounge of a hotel where an insurance convention is being held, intent on causing trouble. He yells, "I think all insurance agents are crooks, and if anyone doesn't like it, come up and do something about it."

Immediately, a man runs up to the drunk and says, "You take that back!"

The drunk sneers, "Why, are you an agent?"

"No," the man replies, "I'm a crook."

CHAPTER 12

What You *Must* Know About Life Settlements

All of sports have a safety net, but boxing is the only sport that has none. So when the fighter is through, he is through. While he was fighting his management was very excited for him, but now that he is done, that management team is moving on.

—Gerry Cooney

Life Settlements

Rest assured, the insurance industry has a solution for you if you can no longer or choose not to continue paying for your life insurance policy. Life insurance settlement companies will happily purchase your policy from your client and provide the client a lump sum payment. Does this sound too good to be true? For many people, it may be.

In 2005 more than $726 billion of life insurance face amount was surrendered. In the same year, $2 trillion of face amount of insurance lapsed. The same trend continued in 2006 through 2008. With this amount of insurance falling off the books in any given year, there may be huge opportunities for senior citizens to benefit from a life settlement, rather than just surrender their policies or walk away. Certainly, from a fiduciary duty perspective, insurance producers, financial planners, and advisors should recognize the potential of the settlement industry to benefit those clients whose policies may qualify.

There are many things that can account for the growth and future potential of the industry, and advisors must better position themselves for that future growth. First of all, there is an increasing awareness of this new market by insurance producers, financial advisors, and tax advisors, which will most certainly bolster the future growth. That, coupled with increasing consumer awareness, will have a positive effect on the growth potential of this concept.

Among the ways to increase awareness of the market is education, not just of the advisors but of the client, so that they are also aware of the potential of their policies in future years. This education process can begin at the point of sale of the policy. Although you cannot predict what the value may be in the future, because of market conditions, health of the insured, and so forth, the advisor can at least show the life settlement as a potential exit strategy for the client in their senior years.

In terms of growth, life settlements represent the fastest growth area of the life insurance industry. In 2004 there was $2.5 billion of death benefit/face amount of life insurance that was transacted via some form of life settlement. In 2005 the amount more than doubled, as it did in 2006. By the end of the year 2007 the amount that was transacted was up to $15 billion of face amount, and projections estimate that in just 10 years, this will be a $160 billion per year industry. As is evident by the above statistics, this is a huge growth industry, and the benefits to the clients may be numerous.

Potential growth in the industry can be highlighted by the fact that only approximately 25 percent of the insurance producers have tried or completed a life settlement. The balance of the producers have either not heard about them or do not feel that they have enough knowledge to properly work with and advise their clients. The challenge is to more effectively educate the financial advisors and point them in the proper direction to shop cases for the benefit of their clients.

Industry Regulation and Compliance

Regulations are fast emerging in the life settlement marketplace, because of the evolving nature of the industry. The National Association of Insurance Commissioners (NAIC) has adopted a Model Act, in which they are establishing guidelines for the life settlement industry. One of the main restrictions is aimed at the STOLI business and premium financed cases going to an intended life settlement, by restricting the sale of a policy to a five-year waiting period from the date of issue of that policy, unless certain conditions are met.

Some reasons that would allow for a sale would be: the insured is terminally ill, the insured's spouse dies, or divorces his or her spouse, or retires. If purchasers want to sell a policy after the two-year contestability period, the guideline is that policy premiums have been funded exclusively with unencumbered assets or with full recourse liability, that there is no agreement or understanding that the liability or purchase of the policy is guaranteed or the loan forgiven, and that the policy has previously not been evaluated for a life settlement. The National Conference of Insurance Legislators (NCOIL) has retained the two-year provision that most of the providers purchasing policies, as well as many of the states that have implemented some form of regulation, have adopted. The NCOIL act is viewed to protect consumer property rights. The Life Insurance Settlement Association (LISA) is continually monitoring the NAIC and NCOIL model acts, and working in all the states that are looking at legislation or adopting provisions from these model acts, to protect the consumer and the life settlement industry.

LISA is involved in clarifying the inner workings of the life settlement industry, and trying to be sure that the states have the appropriate facts in attempting to pass regulations. As of early 2009, there are about 27 states that are looking at different types of legislation to regulate the life settlement industry and to specifically restrict STOLI. Much of the STOLI legislation is, to some extent, putting restrictions on life settlements and the consumer who may have legitimate life settlement and premium financed cases. This is an ever-changing landscape, as many regulators do not understand how the life settlement market really works day to day, yet they are making rules that the industry has to work under. LISA is busy on many fronts, working to uphold where the industry is going. Much of the proposed regulation is also directed toward requiring compensation and other disclosures to the clients. This move toward full disclosure is to create a fully transparent environment for the clients, so sellers know exactly what the disposition of their policies involves.

Licensing and Reporting

Currently there are 29 states that have life settlement regulations in place, and that number is increasing as the new states pass new regulations and the states that have regulations continue to refine what they do as part of their regulation process. This regulation has also imposed licensing requirements and guidelines with which those who wish to conduct a life settlement need to comply.

Some states have mandated that the person effecting the transaction needs to hold a life insurance license. Others have established a specific life settlement broker's license, without the life insurance requirement, and still others have some combination of both. Part of the reason for the specific licensing is to be able to identify those who are participating in the industry, and part is to be able to effectively be sure that the specific guidelines for the settlement industry are being adhered to. This is also reinforced by the fact that many states have reporting requirements that compel both life settlement providers and life settlement brokers to submit a report to the state detailing all life settlement transactions conducted in the state in a given year, and disclosing the name of the financial advisor, seller of the policy, policy details, and compensation paid to all parties. It is the opinion of many that this report is a tool used to monitor potential abuses, and to be sure that the parties are appropriately licensed in the governing state.

Compensation

Industry compensation guidelines are being adopted by more and more providers and brokers, because it seems that the abuses that have taken place in this emerging market have revolved mostly around compensation. A guideline that is increasingly being promoted and has been adopted by a growing number of providers is 6 percent of the face amount of insurance or one-third of the offer amount above cash surrender value, whichever is less. That is a guideline for fixed life insurance policies.

The Financial Industry Regulatory Authority (FINRA), which is the regulatory body formed in 2007 by combining the National Association of Securities Dealers (NASD) and the U.S. Securities and Exchange Commission (SEC), issued a guideline in 2007 that said that for variable life settlement cases, the comp should be 5 percent of the offer amount, closely following compensation rules for securities transactions. The argument is that this is not a realistic level of compensation for this type of transaction, and FINRA is reviewing the guideline. In the meantime, broker–dealers have adopted their own compensation levels with some guidelines to fall somewhere between what FINRA has stated and what seems to be an industry norm for fixed cases. A compromise compensation amóunt for variable policies that might be acceptable is 20 percent of the offer amount, adjusted down if the producer is earning additional commissions from other products sold from the life settlement proceeds. This is all evolving, however.

Compensation Abuse

As with any industry, but particularly with a new industry such as the life settlement industry, there are abuses by the few that have long-reaching effects on the many. In the life settlement industry, the most prevalent abuse has been in compensation. Because there were no regulations on compensation, and because there was not full disclosure or transparency when the life settlements first became popular, some advisors were taking a much larger share of the overall offer than would seem fair or proper.

An example of compensation abuse might look like this:

- Female client age 80, with a Life Expectancy (LE) of seven years
- $3 million universal life insurance policy with no cash surrender value
- Gross offer to purchase the policy was $1.1 million
- The agent wanted to give the client $500,000, saying that the client would have received nothing had she surrendered her policy
- For getting her $500,000 when she would have received nothing, the producer felt that he was entitled to $600,000

This is an extreme example of compensation abuse, but one that is not far the norm. Because there were no rules on the levels of compensation, and because there was no transparency of the transaction or compensation disclosure, abuses like this did happen.

It is because of this type of abuse that many states have implemented compensation disclosure guidelines. The reasoning is that abuses would be minimized if the client knew what the advisor was going to take, and negotiate it or find a new advisor if the amount was out of line. For this reason many of the providers and funding sources buying the policies have dictated the compensation by implementing compensation guideline maximums that fall within the 6 percent of face amount or one-third of the offer amount above cash surrender value, whichever is less, for any of the cases that they purchase.

Other abuses have dealt with fraud or forgery at many levels: fraud at the time of the policy's purchase by insured, insurance agent, and the life insurance carrier, where the facts presented to the carrier were misstated or misleading, giving way to larger amounts of insurance or better rates than might otherwise have been qualified. It is for this reason that life settlement brokers, and more specifically, life settlement providers have fraud-prevention practices that check and recheck information and timelines, to be sure that there are no reasons that the insurance carrier could contest or rescind a policy.

Suitability

Another area of concern has to be suitability of a life settlement transaction. Typically, the suitability forms are required by broker–dealers in variable life transactions, but it would not hurt to complete or at least consider the answers to some questions in evaluating whether to submit a case for a life settlement transaction. Some of the questions might be:

- Does the need for originally purchasing the insurance still exist? If not, what has changed to prompt the sale of the policy? If the need for originally purchasing the policy still does exist, what is the insured doing to offset that need if the policy is sold?

- Has the client considered other options other than the sale of the policy? Are there other potential sources of revenue that the client can tap into to help with the income or cash need that the client is experiencing?

- Has the client been provided with a sample valuation form to help with the decision to go forward? Prior to moving forward with the time and expense of a life settlement, it is always a good idea to evaluate the potential pricing offers that would be received, to be sure that if offers are in that range, the client will be willing to sell the policy.

- Has the client considered the potential tax consequences of selling their policy? There are tax consequences that will be covered later. In considering the consequences, it is important to know what the potential net value of the transaction will be, and what effect it will have on their entire tax picture.

- Is the client aware that the policy being sold still counts toward their insurance-buying capacity? All life insurance companies utilize purchase and in-force guidelines that they employ as part of their underwriting process. Whether a policy is owned by the insured, if it is a force on their life, and it would continue to be in a life settlement transaction, it still counts as part of the insurance-buying capacity that their life holds.

- Is the client aware that there will be ongoing health inquiries by the policy purchaser? Upon the sale of a policy in a life settlement transaction, the insured and/or a named contact will have to provide, in most cases, a quarterly update as to the residence location and health status of the insured. Typically, this update is provided by a relative, legal advisor, or trustee to the purchaser of the policy by sending a postcard or letter as a reply to the purchaser's inquiry.

■ Did the client seek and/or obtain the advice of their financial advisors? In all cases, the client should seek the advice of their financial advisor and legal advisor before completing a life settlement transaction. In addition, the family members and beneficiaries of the client's policy and estate should also be informed of what the client's wishes are before completing the transaction.

Some additional questions that life settlement brokers or producers, or financial advisors should ask are:

■ Do you feel that the client is of sound mental capacity? The majority of the purchasers of life settlement transactions request a certification of competency of the insured client and any owner and trustee involved in making the decision to sell the policy.

■ Given their financial situation, does the life settlement meet the client's objectives? In all situations, a life settlement should be to the client's financial advantage, and the advisor should be working toward meeting whatever the client's objectives are when moving the process forward for a life settlement.

■ Was the life settlement evaluation based on current information? In all cases the medical information should include all medical treatments and evaluations that the client has received prior to obtaining the life expectancy (LE) reports. In addition, the life expectancy reports should be within 90 days of their review date when submitting a file for evaluation. Plus, any insurance company illustrations should be within 90 days, and preferably 30 days, when underwriting and pricing a policy. Anything any older for any of the above could have information that is no longer valid, and could affect the pricing and ultimate completion of the transaction.

- Does the transaction comply with all applicable state regulations? Depending on the state, there are certain guidelines that have been put in place to protect the consumer and the integrity of the transaction. It is imperative that those guidelines be adhered to so that the transaction does not get rejected in the 11th hour due to compliance issues.

- Is the producer–broker-dealer properly licensed? The producer, in regulated states, must adhere to the licensing laws of that state for conducting a life settlement transaction. In addition, it is important to work with a broker who has the compliance systems and knowledge in place to verify licensing, and the use of state-approved sales materials in conducting the life settlement transaction. When conducting variable life settlement transactions, it is also important that the broker–dealer be both securities licensed and life settlement licensed in the states that require these licenses.

Best Execution and Due Diligence

Because of the regulations put forth in many states, the abuses that have taken place, and just a general sense of being sure to dot every "i" and cross every "t," most firms, including the financial advisor, the life settlement broker, and the life settlement provider all have a due diligence process that they implement to be confident that everything is done properly and above board. The due diligence process takes into account a review of procedures for fraud prevention, anti-money laundering, and proper licensing.

The process also takes into account what confidentiality practices there are for the providers purchasing policies, and the procedures necessary to comply with FINRA and broker–dealer requirements when variable life insurance policies are transacted. In addition, firms should practice "best execution" as detailed in the NASD Rule 2320, which says that "the core duty pursuant to the best execution obligation is to use reasonable diligence first to ascertain the best market for the security, and then to obtain the most favorable price possible in that market under prevailing market conditions. Price is only one component of best execution. Other factors include the speed and quality of executing the transaction, and the reliability of other market participants."

When firms attempt to sell a life insurance policy in a life settlement transaction, the firm should make an effort to obtain bids from multiple licensed providers, typically secured through life settlement brokers, to assure that the offer is the best available through multiple sources. This is part of a process that will assure the client that there was due diligence in the life settlement process, to obtain the best available price for the policy.

Fraud Prevention

Most of the entities that are working in the life settlement market have some form of anti-fraud policy in effect. The most efficient way of handling this is to have an anti-fraud committee that can follow through with the checks and balances of a life settlement transaction, to be reasonably sure that there has not been any fraud, but to also have a process in place to address what needs to be done if there has been fraud. Firms, in order to reduce the risk of fraud when settling a life insurance policy, have developed a process of gathering the necessary information and documents, to move things forward, and if they cannot obtain the necessary documentation, the firm will not move forward with the transaction. Some of that documentation includes:

- Current street address and photo identification of the insured and policy owner
- Copy of a signed and dated verification of coverage from the issuing insurance company
- An original or complete copy of the life insurance policy
- A copy of the signed application of the original insurance policy that was issued
- The original or a copy of the entire life settlement application
- A complete physician's report on the insured's current health status
- A current statement by the insured's physician attesting to the competency of the insured who enters into a life settlement contract
- Laboratory reports and supporting physician notes

In addition, document inconsistencies can also indicate possible fraud. Some of these document inconsistencies could include:

- Alterations to forms such as whiteouts, erasures, strikeouts, different inks, or inconsistent handwriting
- Out-of-date information
- Dates on life insurance applications that do not coincide with the medical records
- Answers on life insurance applications that do not coincide with the medical records
- Inconsistencies in statements among insured, agent, physician, and policy owner
- Altered or incomplete medical records
- Obvious inconsistency in signatures

- Lack of physician's signature on letter of competency form, physician's questionnaire and/or diagnosis date confirmation
- Photocopied forms where a typed portion is clearer than the balance of the text

Some activity indicators of fraud in a life settlement transaction could include:

- Disagreement of the insured's health status by the attending physicians
- Withdrawal of a life settlement application by an owner or insured after questions are raised by the broker or provider on a specific case
- An owner or insured who will not provide proof of a current residential address and telephone number
- An owner or insured who becomes evasive or becomes irate about questions pertaining to a life settlement application
- An owner or insured who has purchased multiple life insurance policies within a short period of time
- An owner or insured who is hesitant to allow direct contact with the life insurance company that issued the policy
- Resubmission of a life settlement application with new or different data by the same agent, owner, or producer of a previously rejected or withdrawn life settlement application
- The insured moves frequently and fails to advise anyone of changing physicians

At the close of a review process by the broker, the purchasing provider will conduct a complete review of all of the documents and executed contracts received from the owner and/or the insurance company. If suspected fraud is identified, the transaction is suspended by the provider and that provider should report the suspected fraud to the appropriate state insurance department and request their guidance.

STOLI

Stranger-Owned Life Insurance (STOLI) is one of the less savory back alleys of the life settlement marketplace. "Enterprising" insurance salespeople have used a combination of blandishments and material inducements to convince select high-net-worth senior citizens to "leverage their insurability" for financial gain. The pitch most often goes something like this: "We'll acquire a $xyz million life insurance policy on you. It won't cost you a dime out of pocket, since we'll use a nonrecourse (or even, more recently a recourse) loan to finance the premiums. You'll have 'free' insurance for a couple of years, and after the two-year contestability period is up, we'll sell your policy in the secondary market for a lot more than you've put into it!"

It does not take much imagination to see the myriad ways an arrangement of this type can go wrong for the insured. State regulators and insurance companies are predisposed toward viewing such transactions as fraudulent. In addition, at the same time that numerous economic and environmental factors have led to an increased number of policies entering the secondary marketplace, the investment capital available to many of the traditional institutional buyers has dried up. The result is significant downward pressure on the market price of many policies, leaving the highly leveraged premium-financed policyholder "upside-down" when they attempt to sell their policies.

STOLI must be distinguished from legitimate premium-financing arrangements. There are a number of good reasons that a client might want to utilize OPM (other people's money) to pay their life insurance premiums. However, entering into such a financing arrangement with the intent to divest oneself of the policy in a relatively short period of time in hopes of a financial windfall is not one of those reasons.

Evaluation and Processing

The financial advisor working with a client should have a clear understanding of the options that the insured can have. The advisor should be able to then review all of the options available to the client to determine the best course of action for the client. Part of the initial process is to be able to educate the client on what a life settlement is, how it works, what is required today and in the future, and to help the client evaluate the risks and rewards, to be able to make an intelligent decision on whether to move forward.

If the client wants to move forward to the evaluation process, the completion of a life settlement qualifier form is the first step. That form will rate the premium-to-face ratios, the cash values, the loans if any, the age of the insured, the amount of insurance, and the health of the insured, all as components of a life settlement case, to determine whether it is worth beginning the process.

If the process shows that the life settlement case is worth pursuing, then the next step is the completion of a life settlement questionnaire. This questionnaire is a snapshot of the entire policy situation, showing all of the components that anyone evaluating the policy for a life settlement would be concerned with. The items listed are name, address, date of birth, and policy information such as the type of policy, premiums, and due dates, owner, and state of ownership, beneficiaries. In addition, doctors seen in the last five years, HIPAA forms, premium financed or not, and much more, which are used in the evaluation and pricing process.

The Health Insurance Portability and Accountability Act (HIPAA) form has to be signed authorizing the release and review of medical records. The medical records are typically provided by the insurance advisor or can be obtained by a medical information copy service, from all of the doctors who have been visited over the previous five year period. Experienced life settlement consultants have access to an internal underwriter who can evaluate the medical records to determine the life expectancy (LE) of the individual, a key component in the pricing process. Determining the estimated life expectancy (LE) and plugging that life expectancy into a pricing model is a value-added service that can help eliminate wasting time and money in the life settlement process. The pricing model will give a range of what potential offers to purchase the policy might bring, to determine whether the case is worth pursuing. Following that path saves time and money in weeding out those cases that just simply do not work for all concerned.

Another key component in the evaluation process is to obtain an in-force illustration of the policy that shows the minimum premium to keep the policy in force until age 100. The illustration for a universal life policy should show the minimum premium necessary to pay, where the coverage runs to age 100, as stated above, and the cash surrender value at that time is $1. The illustration should be run using current interest rates and current mortality assumptions.

For variable universal life policies, the illustration should be run as above, using the fixed interest rate bucket of the variable contract. If the policy is a term policy, there are two illustrations that should be run. One illustration should show the term insurance premiums necessary to keep the policy in force, as term insurance, for as long as it will last as term insurance, or to age 90 if possible. The other illustration should be one converting the term insurance to a universal life policy, using the guidelines listed above.

The next step in the process is to send the medical information to two or more approved life expectancy evaluation firms, where they will review all of the medical information and underwrite the medical information to determine the estimated life expectancy, in months, of that individual. The evaluation is done in months, as indicated, and shows several probabilities of death occurring different levels, in months, that are used; that is, 50 percent, or 85 percent chance of death occurring by that estimated time.

The process also has several areas that are key to getting a case processed smoothly. First, the producer has to be appropriately licensed in the state of jurisdiction for the case. The state of jurisdiction is typically the state where the owner resides or the trust is domiciled. Some states do not have any licensing requirements, others have a registration that has to be completed, some specify that there at least has to be a life insurance license, and many have a life settlement or viatical license that has to be obtained for the resident state of the agent and in the state of jurisdiction for the case. This is typically verified and either in place or fulfilled during the entire process.

Once the life expectancy reports are received, then the case is packaged and sent to the life settlement providers whose purchase parameters the case fulfills. The providers then review the medical records, LE reports, and illustrations, and anything else associated with the case, and will make an offer or decline. The best offer is negotiated between all of the providers until there is acceptance of that offer. When the offer is accepted, there is a verification of coverage with the insurance carrier, to be sure that the proper assumptions were used in the entire evaluation process. During that process, contracts are requested from the purchaser, and those are completed by the seller, the financial advisor, and the life settlement broker. Once the purchaser receives the entire contract package including supporting documentation, it is reviewed and a deficiency list is created to address anything that is missing. That is then submitted, and the entire contract is reviewed by the purchaser and their legal team for completeness and accuracy, and when that has taken place, the purchaser will put the funds in escrow.

As soon as the funds are placed in escrow, the purchaser sends the required forms to the life insurance company to change the ownership of the policy from the current owner to the new owner purchasing the policy. This process can take anywhere from a day to several weeks, depending on the life insurance company. When the change of ownership is recorded at the life insurance carrier, the provider is notified and the funds that are being held in escrow can be released to the seller of the contract. There may be a period of time that is either state or provider imposed, where the seller can rescind the transaction and retain possession of the policy, effectively reversing the transaction. Depending on the governing entity, it can be up to 15 days and in some cases, up to 30 days to exercise the option.

Tax Treatment

Up until April 30, 2009, there had been no specific IRS ruling on the tax consequences of the life settlement transaction. There is conventional thinking from advisors that has been readily adopted by those operating in the life settlement market. The tax treatment that is being put forth follows that of life insurance in general, that there is no tax to the cost basis of the policy, ordinary income tax to the cash surrender value (just as if a life insurance policy were surrendered), and long-term capital gains over the cash surrender value. Using this logic, the treatment of the proceeds is exactly the same as if the life insurance policy is surrendered, and has the extra tax on the gain over the cash surrender value, which is a capital gain tied to the gain received from the sale of the contract to an investor. Thus it is viewed as a gain in an investment transaction.

For example, let us assume there was a $1 million policy with $100,000 in cash surrender value, and further assume that the cost basis was $60,000. In shopping the policy for a life settlement to obtain the best price to sell it, an offer was received of $250,000 to sell the policy, of which $50,000 was paid in compensation. The remaining $200,000 would be paid to the seller–owner. The tax picture using the above guideline is that there would be no tax on the first $60,000 of the $200,000 offer amount, ordinary income tax in the client's tax bracket (assume 25 percent) on the next $40,000, and currently 15 percent capital gains tax on the remaining $100,000. Thus, the net to the client would be $175,000 after all taxes. This is a 75 percent increase over the cash surrender value, before any taxes would have been paid on the policy surrender proceeds. If you look at the net value after taxes if the policy was surrendered, there would be no tax on the first $60,000 (cost basis), and ordinary income tax on the next $40,000 (at the same 25 percent rate), netting $90,000 after taxes. Thus, the life settlement transaction produced a net gain of $85,000 to the owner–seller of the contract, over and above the net after-tax gain to the client.

However, on May 1, 2009, the IRS issued a pair of revenue rulings that significantly clarify the state of U.S. federal tax law applicable to transactions involving life insurance policies, including life settlements. Life settlements are a rapidly growing asset category in which investors purchase life insurance policies on the secondary market with the intention of profiting by either reselling them later for a gain or holding them until maturity. One of the impediments to the development of this asset class has been the uncertainty of the U.S. federal income taxation in this area because most of the cases and rulings predate the development of an active secondary market for life insurance policies.

Revenue Ruling 2009–13

In Revenue Ruling 2009–13, the IRS concludes that under Section 721 the original holder of a life insurance contract (the

"Insured") who surrenders the contract for its cash surrender value recognizes ordinary income. The amount of the income is reduced by the sum of all premiums paid under the policy.

The revenue ruling goes on to contrast a surrender of a life insurance policy with a sale of the policy on the secondary market. The amount of the gain on a secondary sale is greater because the IRS concluded that the basis of the life insurance contract should be reduced by the amount expended for the cost of mortality protection before the sale. Additionally, the IRS held that the character of the income in a secondary sale is bifurcated. A portion of the gain, up to the amount of ordinary income that would result from a surrender of the policy, is treated as ordinary income, with the balance of the gain, if any, treated as either long-term or short-term capital gain, depending on the holding period. In the case of a term-life insurance policy, the IRS assumed that absent other proof, the entire premium is used for current insurance protection and thus does not create basis in the policy. Thus, when a term-life insurance contract is sold, the entire amount of the sale proceeds generally will be taxable as capital gain.

Revenue Ruling 2009–14

Revenue Ruling 2009–14 describes the U.S. federal income tax consequences to the person who purchases a term-life insurance contract on the secondary market (the "Secondary Purchaser") upon the receipt of death benefits, or upon the receipt of sale proceeds, with regard to a term-life insurance contract that the Secondary Purchaser sells for profit. The IRS held that on maturity of the life insurance policy, the Secondary Purchaser is required to recognize as income the difference between (1) the total death benefit received and (2) the amount of actual value of the consideration paid for the purchase plus the monthly premiums paid by the Secondary Purchaser. The entire amount of the income is treated as ordinary income. The revenue ruling also held that if the Secondary Purchaser sells the term-life insurance contract to an unrelated party, the entire amount of gain is capital gain. The amount of the gain realized is the excess of the amount realized over the adjusted basis. The adjusted basis is computed as the amount paid to acquire the life insurance contract plus the monthly premiums that were paid to prevent the contract from lapsing.

As described below, because this ruling only applies to term-life contracts, it is unclear if the IRS would allow capitalization (or capital gain treatment) of the entire premium for contracts with cash surrender value. The IRS also held that the death benefit of a life insurance policy written by a U.S. insurance company on the life of a U.S. person is U.S. source income. The IRS ruled that the Secondary Purchaser must recognize ordinary income from sources within the United States, and tax is imposed under Section 881(a)(1) (withholding tax) with respect to this amount

The reduction of basis for the "cost of insurance" for policies sold by the insured is inconsistent with some IRS guidance and several court decisions. The IRS also does not cite any statutory basis in support of its position.

Examples and Application of Revenue Ruling 2009–13

Revenue Ruling 2009–13 addresses and discusses three different fact patterns. For elucidation purposes, please follow this format. Situation 1 will focus on a taxpayer who originated a cash value life insurance policy and later surrenders that policy for the cash surrender value (CSV), while Situation 2 will use the same type of life insurance policy, but rather than surrendering it for the CSV, the taxpayer will sell it to a third party. Lastly, Situation 3 will discuss the tax impacts on the sale of a no cash value life insurance policy (term life).

SITUATION 1   In this situation, the taxpayer purchased a cash value life insurance policy. Eight years later, the taxpayer surrendered the policy for the CSV of $78,000, which reflects a $10,000 subtraction for the cost-of-insurance (COI) charges. During the period of ownership, the taxpayer paid premiums totaling $64,000 and the taxpayer neither received distributions nor borrowed against the CSV.

Tax Holding   The taxpayer recognized $14,000 of income on the surrender of the contract, which is determined by subtracting the CSV ($78,000) from the investment in the contract ($64,000). The $14,000 gain is taxed as ordinary income.

Rule for surrender by original policy owner:
- Determine basis by calculating the investment in the contract (cumulative premiums paid)
- The gain is amount by which cash surrender value exceeds basis
- The gain is taxed at ordinary income

SITUATION 2   In this situation, the facts are the same as Situation 1 except that the taxpayer sells the insurance policy to a third party, who would suffer no economic loss upon the death of the insured, in the eighth year for $80,000.

Tax Holding   The taxpayer realized $80,000 from the sale of the insurance policy. The basis in the contract is $54,000, which reflects the investment in the contract ($64,000) minus the COI ($10,000). Therefore, the taxpayer recognizes $26,000 upon the sale of the contract ($80,000–$54,000). $14,000 of the recognized amount is taxed as ordinary income ($78,000 CSV less $64,000 aggregate premiums paid) and the remaining $12,000 is taxed as long-term capital gain.

Rule for sale by original policy owner:

- Calculate the basis by subtracting the cumulative COI charges from the investment in the contract (cumulative premiums paid)
- The gross income on the sale of the contract is the amount by which the sales price exceeds the basis
- The portion of the gain up to the amount by which the cash surrender value exceeds the basis is ordinary income
- The balance of the gain is capital gain

SITUATION 3   The facts in this situation are the same as the other two situations except that the life insurance contract is a zero cash value term life insurance policy. The monthly premium is $500; the taxpayer has paid premiums of $45,000 over the period of the contract. Eight years into the contract, the taxpayer sold the policy to a third party for $20,000.

Tax Holding   Absent any proof to the contrary, the COI equals the premium. Assuming the taxpayer sold the policy in the middle of the month and the taxpayer had prepaid the premium, the basis in the contract equals the prorated prepaid premium—in this case, $250. The taxpayer recognized $19,750 of gain on the sale of the insurance policy. Given that the policy had no inside CSV buildup and the taxpayer held the policy for more than one year, the gain is categorized as long-term capital gain.

Rule for term policies:

- The basis of a term policy is zero, except for prepaid premium
- For example, on a policy for which an annual premium has been paid, but is sold mid–policy year, the basis would be one-half the annual policy premium

- The amount by which the sales price exceeds the basis is capital gain

COMMENTS   Although this is the first revenue ruling issued with regard to life settlements, it leaves some unanswered questions. Nevertheless, it provides at least some tax guidance for the more standard settlements. This revenue ruling will not "be applied adversely to sales occurring before August 26, 2009."

If you ever get a touch of insomnia and turn your television on at 2 A.M., between the magic pasta maker and super sharp slicing knife infomercials you are likely to see ads for life settlements. Many commercials show an insurance policy owner screaming, "I want my money now!" Oh, the life settlement companies will give you your money now—you just may not like what they give you.

Many life settlement companies will pay your client an amount greater than the cash surrender value in the policy, but less than the full amount of the death benefit... much less. Payments will often range from 10 percent to 30 percent of the death benefit (face amount).[1]

Life settlements present a moral dilemma. A financial services company has just paid you 20 percent (for example) of the death benefit of the policy to become the new owner and beneficiary of your policy. The company pays your client's policy every year and waits from days to decades until your client dies, when they collect the life insurance proceeds.

Much of the money funding the life settlement industry comes from private hedge funds and wealthy private investors who are disinterested parties looking for the best returns on their investments.

What are the alternatives to entering into a life settlement?[2] There are several options to consider:

- Borrow against the cash value of your life insurance policy
- Cash out the policy based on the available cash surrender value
- Check with the life insurance company to find out if the policy can be converted to a paid-up policy or if the death benefit can be reduced in order to lower the amount of the premium payments
- Use the life insurance policy as collateral to secure a loan

If whole life insurance is an appropriate solution for your needs, evaluate all your client's options before canceling or selling the policy. You would not want to make a poor decision on an expensive insurance policy and potentially be disqualified from purchasing a replacement policy in the future due to financial constraints or because you have become uninsurable.

Case Studies

Case studies are helpful to the advisor to show how a life settlement could develop, and the value to the client. These studies are intended to show the value to the client, as mentioned, but also to demonstrate the many different situations that life settlements offer a practical and profitable solution for the client and the advisor. The tax obligations in these actual case studies were prior to the new revenue rulings issued by the IRS on May 1, 2009.

Case Study #1

The first case represents an estate planning sale that was completed in 2000, in which there was a $3 million policy written on a 74 year old, with an annual premium of $81,000. In 2000, the estate tax exclusion was $600,000 per person. With the new tax bill that had passed, by the year 2006, the estate tax exclusion was $2,000,000 per person. For a married couple, the $4,000,000 of total exclusion and the reduction in the tax rate from 55 percent to 45 percent, basically eliminated the need to continue to carry the coverage (subject to the tax cut being made permanent). In 2006 the client was 80 years old, and the CSV was $10,000. The policy received a gross offer of $960,000, which represented 32 percent of the death benefit. Gross compensation was $180,000, split between the producer and the broker. The policy owner received $780,000. The insured's cost basis, for income tax purposes, was $486,000. Taxes were $44,100, or 15 percent of $294,000 (the difference between the owner's gross proceeds of $787,000 and cost basis of $486,000). That left the owner's, after taxes, with $735,900. This is much better than the $10,000 they would have received if the policy was surrendered.

Case Study #2

A 72-year-old man had $4.8 million of life insurance in force on his life. He was living on income from a small business and Social Security, and some investment and Individual Retirement Account (IRA) proceeds. He had to close his small business and needed to find some income to supplement what he was currently receiving. Of the $4.8 million of life insurance on his life, $1.5 million was term insurance, nearing the end of the time frame where he could convert it to universal life, and to when the term period would expire. In reviewing everything with his advisor, the owner–insured of the policy decided he wanted to explore what the policy would generate in a life settlement transaction. In shopping the policy, the advisor presented a conversion universal life illustration to the providers that would look at the policy. The policy was ultimately settled for a $214,000 offer net to the client. In converting and selling the term policy, which had no value and would be expiring in two years, the client received $214,000. This money was helpful to offsetting the income needs that the client was experiencing and still left $3.3 million of life insurance in force on his life.

Case Study #3

In December 2008, an insured had experienced some changes in the value of his estate and no longer wanted to pay premiums on his $10,000,000 universal life insurance policy. The insured was 81 years old, and had an estimated average life expectancy (LE) of 116 months. The annual premium on the policy was approximately $680,000, and the cash surrender value was $0. The financial advisor, when approached about surrendering the policy, suggested to the trustee that before cancelling the policy they should explore the life settlement market to see if the policy would hold any value in that type of transaction. After submitting all the requirements to the providers whose parameters the case fit, the client received $1,400,000 for the policy. A savvy advisor helped his client create $1,400,000 from the life settlement transaction that they otherwise would never have received.

Case Study #4

There was an insured who was insured with key man life insurance policies in three businesses in which he was a part owner. Each policy was for $10,000,000 of term insurance. He was in his mid-seventies and wanted to buy out his partner in one of the businesses. His financial advisor suggested using one of the policies to see what the value in a life settlement transaction would generate. His life expectancy (LE) was 97 months. The advisor obtained an illustration for each of the policies showing the conversion to a universal life insurance policy and the policies were shopped to more than 45 providers. There were offers made of approximately $3,100,000 per policy, net to the owner. The client used the proceeds from two of the policies, after the taxes were paid, plus other cash he had and minimal loans, to buy his partner's share of one of the businesses. It was a situation where there was term insurance with no current cash value, and produced more than $5,600,000 of cash after taxes, from the life settlement transaction that made the deal possible.

Case Study #5

A 78-year-old female with a substantial estate (in excess of $250 million) had approximately $120 million of life insurance in force for estate planning and charitable-giving purposes. She had established a charitable gift of $50 million of insurance for a school that wanted to construct a new building. The school had asked her to donate money now rather than receiving the money at her death. Rather than give money from her estate today, she evaluated selling $25 million of her life insurance as a life settlement. Based on her life expectancy and the premiums on the policies, there was a net offer to the client's trust of $8 million, which was given to the school along with a promise to pay the equivalent of the premiums on the policies for the two years that they expected to build the property. It was a situation that allowed them to use her insurance to create the proceeds necessary to effect the construction of the new school building.

Case Study #6

A trustee of an estate had a $2 million policy on an 82-year-old male who had purchased the policy in 1994. The trust had been funding the policy with minimum premiums to keep it in force.

136

In 2007 the premiums to be paid were significantly higher than they were when it was first purchased, because interest rates were less than half of what they were when the policy was purchased, and the increased mortality cost of the insured. The required premium was $47,000 in that year and would increase each year, and there was virtually no cash value in the policy. The insured had the normal health issues of someone age 82, and when doing a life expectancy evaluation, it was estimated to be eight years. A new life insurance policy for $2 million was underwritten and would cost $78,000 for next 12 years. The original life insurance policy was shopped and sold for $725,000 to the trust. The cost basis of the original policy was $465,000, and when calculating the net to the client after tax, it came to $686,000. This $686,000 was sufficient to pay for the new policy beyond the client's current estimated life expectancy.

Case Study #7

An insured female, age 83, had $1.25 million of life insurance in force, with approximately $180,000 in cash surrender value. She had other insurance and wanted to eliminate the need to pay premiums on this policy. The provider that was interested in the policy had two types of offers to make. One offer was a flat $400,000 for the policy, of which the client would receive $360,000 after the financial advisor and life settlement broker were paid. The other offer was an option for the client to have a paid-up death benefit of $850,000, with $20,000 in compensation paid to the financial advisor and life settlement broker. The client opted for the paid-up policy, which still gave them their tax-free death benefit, but on a reduced basis, and the provider offering this option would receive the balance of the death benefit when the client died. This is a new pricing option that several of the more sophisticated funding sources are offering for the policies today.

Fiduciary Duty Case Study

Another example is an estate planning case that did not happen. Nicholas M. Mallis, CLU, Fallston, Maryland, relates the following, which further emphasizes the fiduciary responsibility of the advisors, in working with their clients.

> *While attending a conference for a financial planning group, I had met an advisor who had a client that had a $5 million second-to-die policy on an 88-year-old couple. The cash surrender value in the policy was $100,000, and the annual premium was $130,000. The couple did not want to carry the insurance anymore because of the change in the estate tax exclusion and the marginal tax rate, and because they did have other insurance, and they felt they really did not need to spend the $130,000 premium. The agent cash-surrendered the policy at their request. The potential for this case could have been a gross offer of over $2 million, maximum total comp of $300,000, and a net to the client of $1.7 million. This is a lot better than the $100,000 that they received. There is a fiduciary responsibility to tell your clients that the secondary market exists, and to do a life settlement evaluation to predetermine the value of a policy before surrendering it.*

Caveat Venditor

Every bit of the preceding information begs our burning question: How do I, as a fiduciary advisor, best advise my clients about life settlements?

Mark Boehm, a Dallas-based insurance advisor experienced in life settlements, emphasizes one of the dangers faced by would-be sellers:

Probably the main issue sellers face is a near total lack of transparency about the financial aspects of the transaction. A seller can and must insist upon full disclosure with regard to the Settlement Offer. Unless the seller "gets it in writing," they have literally no idea regarding the amount of the original dollar offers from purchasers, how much commission the agent is pocketing, the amount of the override the agent's MGA (Managing General Agent) is keeping, how much money the broker who found the Buyer is retaining. ...The list of potential parties with their fingers in the till is pretty long.

The dangers to the consumer associated with selling an existing life insurance policy into the life settlements marketplace mirror, in many ways, the hazards attendant with buying the policy in the first place. Only in this case, it is "Seller Beware"!

Summary

For a host of reasons, a policyholder might be inclined to either surrender their insurance policy, or simply allow it to lapse. Oft-cited reasons include a lack of resources with which to pay the premiums, and no extant need for the insurance as financial planning needs shift. Rather than surrender the policy to the insurance company for its cash surrender value, an advisor might suggest looking into a life settlement as an alternative.

Regulation of the industry is a patchwork of more and less effective state-by-state oversight. Some states require licensing of insurance agents involved in facilitating life settlement transactions. Some do not. Policy purchasers may or may not be subject to licensing requirements and/or state oversight.

Similarly, settlement brokers are more or (usually) less regulated. How a consumer fares in this bazaar is, as is the case with life insurance in general, almost entirely contingent on the level of expertise of the advisor with whom they become involved.

Arguably, an advisor acting in a fiduciary capacity would be compelled not only to counsel their client about the option to settle versus surrender, but to help navigate them through the byzantine process of settlement itself. Unless the advisor is intimately familiar with life settlement transactions, this responsibility can be problematic. One solution is a referral to a life settlement consultant with the expertise to evaluate management alternatives for the existing policy, shop for and evaluate settlement offers in the secondary market (or engage and oversee the brokers who do so), and make recommendations and explain alternatives as a result of the preceding activities. Again, documentation of the process, as well as complete transparency with respect to the financial specifics of the alternatives is paramount.

Profound Insight #12

A stockbroker was cold-calling about a penny stock and found a taker. "I think this one will really move," said the broker. "It's only $1 a share." "Buy me 1,000 shares," said the client. The next day the stock was at $2. The client called the broker and said, "You were right, give me 5,000 more shares." The next day the client looked in the paper and the stock was at $4. The client ran to the phone and called the broker, "Get me 10,000 more shares," said the client. "Great!" said the broker. The next day the client looked in the paper and the stock was at $9. Seeing what a great profit he had in just a few days, the client ran to the phone and told the broker, "Sell all my shares!" The broker said, "To whom? You were the only one buying that stock."

Notes

1. IMS Settlements, LLC, www.imssettlements.com/case-examples .asp.

2. New York State Department of Insurance, "Life Settlements—Top Ten Questions," www.ins.state.ny.us/que_top10/que_life_set.htm.

CHAPTER 13

What Health Insurance Agents "Forget" to Tell Their Clients

I was painfully initiated into boxing, because the guys I fought were a lot bigger than me.

—*Sugar Ray Leonard*

Out of Control Costs

Imagine a health insurance agent speaking with your business client about their health insurance. The agent is thinking about the $100,000 premium they are going to receive when your client renews his major medical health insurance plan. The agent conveniently forgets to mention an alternative type of health insurance plan that can reduce premiums by 40 percent—a Health Savings Account (HSA).

Think this is not happening every day? Think again.

If you think rising health-care costs are only the insurance company's problem or your employer's problem, think again. Most employees pay 10 percent to 90 percent of their health-care costs, when all costs are included. All it takes is a quick review of your pay stub over the last few years to see that the insurance companies are passing on increasing health-care costs to employers and employers are passing on these costs to employees. Health-care costs have risen 8 percent to 10 percent each year over the last three years and are likely to grow two to three times the rate of inflation for the foreseeable future.

Compounding the problem are state insurance laws. Almost every state in the United States can deny individuals coverage through the underwriting process. New Jersey is one of only five states in the United States that provides for "guaranteed issue"—which guarantees health coverage, regardless of health status, age, claims history, or any other risk factor. Although this may be considered a blessing, it is an expensive blessing. Almost by definition, this increases the cost of insurance coverage for everyone in the state to account for those who use the benefits most.

Established as part of the Medicare Prescription Drug, Improvement, and Modernization Act of 2003, the HSA is a hybrid between health insurance and a retirement plan. The HSA was established so savings used for qualified medical expenses for yourself or anyone you claim as a spouse or dependent would be free from taxes. Qualified medical expenses include medical doctors, dental and optical care, chiropractic care, long-term care, and Medicare Part A or Part B, and Medicare HMO insurance premiums. Unqualified medical expenses include cosmetic surgery, health club dues, nonprescription drugs and medicines, and funeral expenses.

Aaron Skloff, AIF, CFA, MBA, CEO of Skloff Financial Group, an investment management and group benefits firm based in Berkeley Heights is an expert on HSAs. "Because the HSA is based on a high deductible insurance plan, the employee takes on a higher level of responsibility and risk for medical expenses than a traditional insurance policy," says Skloff.

He explains that employees who run their family to the doctor office every time someone has the sniffles (because the visit only costs them $10, while the insurance company pays the remaining $65 under a traditional plan) will think twice when they pay the full $75 out of their own pocket under an HSA.

That said, those out-of-pocket costs are all with pretax dollars that were contributed to the HSA. By utilizing an HSA employers can reduce their premium costs by as much as 50 percent, passing most or all of those savings directly to the employees. Many employers, particularly in "guaranteed issue" states like New Jersey, are implementing an HSA based on these benefits.

According to Michael N. Kessler, MD, MA, president of K&L Agency, a benefits consulting firm located in Freeport, New York:

> *While HSA-HDHPs [Health Savings Account—High Deductible Health Plan] can prove to be the answer for maintaining quality health-care and health insurance for some businesses, far too many small businesses enroll their employees in these plans without adequate investigation, preparation or ancillary services. When this occurs, employee satisfaction plummets, anticipated cost savings are not realized, absenteeism worsens, and ultimately [employee] retention suffers as employees receive some of the poorest quality care. These risks are minimal in mid-sized companies and essentially nonexistent in large-sized companies due to their diverse demographics.*

To avoid these pitfalls, any size company must have in place prior to the institution of an HSA-HDHP, a quality disease management and wellness program, and substantial amounts of education provided to employees using various formats (e.g., meetings, literature, videos) offered multiple times. Benefit managers must obtain a detailed list of qualifying preventive services from the health insurance carrier (i.e., the list of services not subject to the employee's deductible) and

145

ensure that all employees understand how to use these services properly.

Employees need to be strongly encouraged to discuss their new health plan with their care providers because some providers are less than enthusiastic about waiting for small payments from each patient rather than large payments from a few insurance carriers. Learning about one's providers' expectations early in the process can help eliminate frustration later.

Small Business at Risk

Even with adequate preparation, some companies' employee demographics do not allow for the expected savings. In particular, companies with a high percentage of families (as opposed to single employees) and employees with chronic diseases may find themselves paying more to use an HSA-HDHP compared with a more traditional plan. The following example demonstrates this scenario for a relatively healthy family of four.

Lance has been working at the ABC Corporation for more than 20 years. As of January 1, 2007, his company is changing their health insurance to an HSA-HDHP. Prior to 2007 Lance had a more traditional plan. His employer paid every employee $250 per month for their insurance coverage (one-half the cost of single coverage) leaving Lance to pay $925 each month. Lance is married with two children. Ten years ago at the age of 46, he was diagnosed with mild coronary artery disease, high blood pressure, and high cholesterol requiring him to take atenolol, Zocor®, and Plavix®. His wife, Torrey, age 51, has suffered from seasonal allergies her entire life and uses Flonase® for about two months each spring. Of the children, Madison, age 17, is healthy and takes no medication while Logan, age 16, has chronic asthma and uses an Aerobid® inhaler daily. Fortunately for Lance, in 2007 his family experienced no serious illnesses, but they all received annual physicals and the appropriate routine tests. First, let us look at his family's medical costs if the family had continued with their more traditional plan (see Exhibit 13.1).

Exhibit 13.1 shows that Lance's total cost for his family's health insurance and health care is $13,130 per year. In this example, we have not considered that his health insurance premiums are collected pretax, thereby saving him additional money. Also, under this more traditional plan, if a family member needs to go to the emergency room, there is a flat co-pay of $75. If a family member requires hospitalization, the co-pay is $500. These same costs are considerably higher under his new HSA-HDHP.

Now let us see what happens to Lance's expenses when his company switches to their new HSA-HDHP plan. Under this new plan, the employer pays every employee $150 per month for their insurance coverage (one-half the cost of single coverage) leaving Lance to pay $650 each month. With this plan, the family must meet a $6,000 deductible and then pay 20 percent of the remaining costs. This deductible does not include the insurance premiums and neither does the plan's $10,000 maximum out-of-pocket expense. Exhibit 13.2 lists the family's new costs.

Thus far, the HSA-HDHP will cost Lance's family slightly more in 2007 ($165) than his more traditional plan. In addition, the maximum amount of money that Lance can contribute to an HSA in 2007 is $5,650. As he will need $4,595 for regular expenses, he will only be left with $1,055 in which to invest in his HSA. (The maximum HSA contribution for a family in 2007 is $5,650.) Finally, what happens if a family member needs to visit the emergency room or requires hospitalization? Recall that under Lance's more traditional plan, he would pay a $75 co-pay for an emergency room visit and a $500 co-pay for hospitalization.

Exhibit 13.1 Details of Lance's Family's Medical Expenses with a More Traditional Plan

Name	Description of Service	Amount Family Pays[1]	Actual Cost of Service[2]
Lance			
	Annual Physical Examination	$20	$185
	EKG and Interpretation	0	225
	Routine Blood Tests	0	210
	4 × 3-month supply of atenolol (G)[3]	80	80
	4 × 3-month supply of Zocor® (F-P)[3]	200	1,600
	4 × 3-month supply of Plavix® (F-NP)[3]	400	1,500
Torrey			
	Annual Physical Examination	$20	$185
	EKG and Interpretation	0	225
	Routine Blood Tests	0	210
	Gynecological Examination and Associated Tests	20	375
	2-month supply of Flonase® (NF)[3]	170	170
Madison			
	Annual Physical	0	215
	Routine Blood Tests	0	145
Logan			
	Annual Physical	0	215
	Routine Blood Tests Plus[4]	0	195
	Routine Follow-up with Allergist	20	295
	4 × 3-month supply of Aerobid® (F-P)[3]	200	950
Health Insurance Premiums × 12 months		**$11,100**	
Total		**$12,230**	**$6,980**

[1]Co-pay for routine office visit; adults $20 per visit and children under age 19 $0 per visit.

[2]Medication costs are national average retail drug store prices per the *Red Book: Pharmacy's Fundamental Reference*, published by Thomson Healthcare, 2007; all other costs represent the national average per the American Medical Association, 2007.

[3]Insurance carrier medication designation and co-pay amounts:

  G = generic medication; $10 per month or $20 per 3-month mail order.

  F-P = on formulary and preferred brand; $25 per month or $50 per 3-month mail order

  F-NP = on formulary but nonpreferred brand; $50 per month or $100 per 3-month mail order

  NF = nonformulary medication; full cost of medication borne by employee

[4]Ted's asthma requires additional blood tests not needed for Mary.

Exhibit 13.2 Details of Lance's Family's Medical Expenses with the HSA-HDHP

Name	Description of Service	Amount Family Pays[1]	Actual Cost of Service[2]
Lance			
	Annual Physical Examination[1]	$0	$185
	EKG and Interpretation[1]	0	225
	Routine Blood Tests[1]	0	210
	4 × 3-month supply of atenolol[3]	80	80
	4 × 3-month supply of Zocor®[3]	1,600	1,600
	4 × 3-month supply of Plavix®[3]	1,500	1,500
Torrey			
	Annual Physical Examination[1]	$0	$185
	EKG and Interpretation[1]	0	225
	Routine Blood Tests[1]	0	210
	Gynecological Examination and associated tests[1]	0	375
	2-month supply of Flonase®[3]	170	170
Madison			
	Annual Physical[1]	0	215
	Routine Blood Tests[1]	0	145
Logan			
	Annual Physical[1]	0	215
	Routine Blood Tests Plus[1]	0	195
	Routine Follow-up with Allergist	295	295
	4 × 3-month supply of Aerobid® (F-P)[3]	950	950
Health Insurance Premiums × 12 months		**$7,800**	
Total		**$12,395**	**$6,980**

[1]Preventive services are covered in full; routine office visits by adults or children require full payment until the deductible is met followed by 20% coinsurance.

[2]Medication costs are national average retail drug store prices per the *Red Book: Pharmacy's Fundamental Reference*, published by Thomson Healthcare, 2007; all other costs represent the National average per the American Medical Association, 2007.

[3]Medications require full payment until the deductible is met followed by 20% coinsurance.

With the new HSA-HDHP, Lance's deductible is $6,000. He would have to pay the first $1,405 of the emergency room bill ($6,000 deductible − $4,595 paid in "regular expenses" = $1,405 deductible remaining) followed by 20 percent of any remaining amount until Lance had paid a total of $10,000 (his maximum out-of-pocket expense). Remember, the $10,000 does not include what he pays in insurance premiums. The same payment would be required for hospitalization. It is easy to see how this typical family could pay thousands more by using an HSA-HDHP.

Consequently, if a majority of employees are likely to meet most of or their entire deductible early in the year, money will probably not be saved by using an HSA-HDHP. This is often the case with single employees who have chronic diseases such as diabetes or with families that usually experience the occasional illness or injury or have stable and mild chronic diseases such as seasonal allergies. Also, subsequent years may become more difficult for these employees as their deductibles will likely increase each year depending on the insurance carrier's annual plan changes.

Trying to budget for these types of expenses can severely hurt an employee's bottom line. Savvy employees might be able to save money by changing from a nonformulary medication to a generic (possibly saving themselves hundreds or even thousands of dollars), but not everyone will be able to do this. Those employees who lack the knowledge, initiative, or ability (i.e., they may not tolerate similar medications) may be required to pay their entire deductible purchasing medication during the first few months of each year. These employees will be prevented from benefiting from the investment of HSA money or through income tax deductibility. Accordingly, it is incumbent on benefit managers to carefully evaluate the effect of an HSA-HDHP on employees prior to its initiation and every year thereafter.

The Risk of On-Site Medical Clinics

Another strategy to control costs that many large- and mid-sized companies are considering involves the institution of an HSA-HDHP along with on-site medical clinics. These on-site medical clinics provide acute care to employees covering everything from a migraine headache or stomachache to blood pressure and wellness screenings. Not having to leave the office saves hours of time while most of these on-site clinics' services are free or provided at minimal cost to employees. As such, health insurance is not involved in these services.

According to a 2005 *Fortune* article, "By giving workers access to convenient medical care . . . [the] company can trim [its] health-care costs from 10 percent to 12 percent. 'When workers don't have to leave the office to get medical care, you cut down on absenteeism and costs,' says [Frank] Martin [of CHD Meridian]. . . . 'You also become an employer of choice by showing that you care about the health of your workers. It's not just talk anymore'" ("A Better Rx for What Ails Us," 2005, *Fortune,* 152, S6–S8).

However, problems might exist with combining an HSA with an on-site medical clinic. According to Dr. Kessler, "The HSA administrative guidelines issued by the IRS suggest that the presence of on-site medical care offered to employees will void the tax deductible status of an HSA plan. In addition, severe penalties are imposed on the employees when an illegal HSA is established—all monies contributed to the HSA will be fully taxed and may be subject to a 10 percent penalty at the discretion of the IRS.

According to a medical director at Pitney Bowes, in off-the-record discussions with the IRS, there are no plans to enforce this rule against companies with on-site medical clinics, but there are no guarantees that this will not change at an unknown time in the future. Without an official policy statement,

151

companies are taking a big risk establishing an HSA with on-site medical centers.

Using an HSA for your Personal Retirement

In past years, the Treasury and IRS dictated that the maximum total contribution to an HSA from all sources had to be the lesser of the in-network deductible or the indexed maximum figures provided by the IRS, and the maximum total contribution from all sources had to be prorated according to the number of full months that an insured was enrolled in an HDHP in a given year.

For example, an individual enrolling in an HDHP on February 1 would only be allowed to contribute eleven-twelfths of the calculated maximum, while an individual enrolling on November 1 would only be allowed to contribute two-twelfths of the calculated maximum for that year.

The purpose of this rule was to prevent wealthy sole proprietors, small business owners, and even corporate executives from enrolling in an HDHP with a high deductible in December of each year, contributing the maximum amount allowable to their HSAs, and cancelling their HDHPs while maintaining traditional coverage the rest of the year. In this way, a new tax-deductible retirement account would become available to those who had maximized their 401(k) contributions and whose incomes disallowed tax-advantaged IRA contributions.

In 2007 both of these rules were eliminated allowing every HSA participant to contribute the maximum allowable amount as defined by the IRS without consideration for the month in which an individual enrolls in an HDHP. However, significant penalties are incurred if the participant is not eligible to participate in the HSA for the entire subsequent 12-month testing period. The ethics of wealthy individuals using their HSA accounts as tax-advantaged retirement accounts is debatable.

What is certain is that if the originally feared exploitation of the HSA tax advantages occurs with excessive frequency, the rule will likely revert to its pre-2007 days, hurting the average employee more than anyone.

Creating an Employee Retirement Vehicle

Contributions made to an HSA on behalf of an eligible insured are deductible on the insured's income tax return "above the line." Contributions made by an employer to an employee's HSA are also excluded from gross income for employment tax purposes. Pursuant to the U.S. Department of Labor (DOL), an employer is permitted to open an HSA account for an employee and deposit funds into that HSA without obtaining the consent of the employee.

Some employers had the idea (and some still do) that establishing HSA accounts for their employees would result in the characterization of the HSA as an ERISA-covered plan allowing employers to establish otherwise prohibited rules for these accounts such as vesting, funding, contribution, and distribution requirements, thereby providing for an employee-funded retirement plan.

The Department of Labor's Field Assistance Bulletin 2004–01 clarified the ERISA rules, stating quite clearly that this is not the case. Any attempt by an employer to impose vesting, funding, contribution, or distribution requirements on any HSA, even making the employer's contribution contingent on any such requirement, is strictly illegal.

IRS Form 8889 (HSA)

Although it may seem obvious, many taxpayers complete IRS Form 8889 (Health Savings Accounts) incorrectly by including nonqualified distributions/expenses. These can include payments for what the taxpayer believes was preventive care, despite the doctor and insurance company coding the visit as a routine visit (i.e., not preventive), and payments for insurance premiums, cosmetic or elective surgeries, funeral expenses, household help, medications purchased from outside the United States (unless authorized by the FDA), and many more.

IRS Publication 502 gives a general description of qualified and nonqualified expenses, but many expenses do not clearly fall into either category. For example, dues to join a health club are deductible as a qualified HSA expense if a doctor recommends the activity due to a person's health problems or obesity. Joining a health club solely to improve one's personal appearance is not a qualified expense. Nevertheless, many taxpayers include nonqualified expenses in their total qualified distributions list on line 13 of Form 8889, and unless audited by the IRS, they will continue to enjoy the benefits of an illegal income tax deduction through their HSAs.

More Effective Strategy

Rising health-care costs have impacted employers of all sizes, however the small business market has been hit the hardest. Larger consumers (of group health-care insurance) are almost by definition able to wield greater negotiating clout than their small business counterparts. In addition, the burden resulting from cost-shifting the care of large numbers of uninsured onto the private sector weighs disproportionately on the small business employer. This explanation is a partial one, however. One of the fundamental reasons for the disproportionate impact on the small business market is a flawed strategy in the approach to purchasing insurance packages from carriers.

The predominant insurance purchasing strategy for small businesses is a premium comparison spread-sheeting approach, with little or no input from the businesses financial function. Using the carrier spread-sheeting approach, a business will have a benefits broker spreadsheet 5 or 10 different benefit carriers to "see who has the best rate this year." Once they have found the best price, they change carriers. The flaw in this strategy is that there is no creative financial input in the process. As a result, benefits purchasing is viewed as a necessary evil and not a strategic business function to be levered for competitive advantage.

Large organizations can better control the continuously accelerating cost impact of health benefits because they treat purchasing as a core strategic function of the company. Their process involves 90- to 120-day RFP (Request for Proposal) submissions, due diligence, risk and financial analysis, and reinsurance negotiations. The larger markets treat insurance as a risk management function, not a necessary evil.

Aggregate Cap Planning

The small business market is simply incapable of replicating these processes due to a lack of internal resources. However, a more sophisticated and increasingly prevalent health-care purchasing strategy (aggregate cap planning) has begun to bring large company risk management processes to the small business market.

To understand aggregate cap planning, you first must understand how insurance is traditionally purchased. The major components of a traditional indemnity medical plan are:

- **Deductible for medical services:** This is the upfront cost the participant must pay before the insurance company starts paying anything toward medical expenses. The deductible generally only applies to inpatient/outpatient types of service, not everyday procedures such as offices visits and prescription benefits.

- **Coinsurance for medical services:** This is the percentage of total claims the participant must pay after they have reached their deductible. This coinsurance generally only applies for inpatient/outpatient types of services, not everyday procedures such as office visits and prescription benefits.

- **Office visit co-pays:** This is usually a token amount of money a participant must pay to see a physician.

- **Prescription benefit card:** This is a token amount of money a participant must pay to fill prescriptions.

There are many other potential facets of plan designs; however, these are the most basic. In a traditional small business insurance purchase, an executive who wants to offer the employees a plan with a $1,000 deductible and an 80 percent rate of coinsurance will submit the requested parameters to a broker. The broker then gathers spreadsheets from carriers that offer plans with these precise characteristics. Once the spreadsheets are gathered, the executive makes a decision on these plans based on a variety of different benchmarks: total cost, network availability, claims payment, and ease of administration. This is for the most part a simple process resulting from the lack of sophistication and lack of understanding about the availability of more sophisticated options displayed by most brokers in the marketplace.

HRA

The concept of aggregate cap planning adds a risk management component into this process. Aggregate cap planning is based on the immutable fact that if you raise the deductible on any given plan, the fixed costs or premiums of that plan will decrease. Couple this with the fact that what the business owner desires is a decrease in the total costs of their benefits, *not* necessarily a decrease in the cost of a particular plan. Do not rethink the carrier, rethink the design. Using this strategy, rather than purchasing the $1,000 plan requested by the executive, a more sophisticated benefits consultant might suggest three designs:

1. Purchase a plan that carries a $5,000 deductible. This will provide a 20 percent to 30 percent reduction in costs relative to the $1,000 plan. This deductible of $5,000 is the "total deductible."
2. Employees will be allocated a deductible of $1,000. This is referred to as the "assigned deductible."
3. The difference between the total and assigned deductibles is referred to as an "implied" deductible. This implied deductible is paid by the employer in the event that an employee incurs charges in excess of their assigned deductible.

This first step in the process is usually accomplished by using an HSA-HDHP coupled with an HRA (Health Reimbursement Arrangement). This simply means that the employer can reimburse employees for deductible expenses on a tax-deductible (to the employer) basis. If we stop the process here, we have saved money. However, we have also created a potential large unfunded liability in the form of an implied deductible for every employee, child, and spouse. For example, in the typical 50-employee firm, there will be approximately 70 participants in the plan (employees, spouses, and children). This benefits restructuring creates a potential liability (in this example) of $4,000 × 70 or $280,000. Further, if the company plan does not renew on January 1 of the year, the actual worst-case liability is then $560,000 because deductibles are on a calendar year not a plan year. Many benefits consultants will get so far as to ensure that the new plan start dates coincide with the calendar year (limiting the implied deductible) and be done with it. The employer saves money, the broker gets a nice commission, everybody's happy.

Mark Boehm, a Dallas-based financial advisor who works with business owners optimizing benefits plan design, offers additional insight. "Three words that very few benefits consultants recognize the significance of, are Managing General Underwriter (MGU). Without knowledge of, access to, and a good working relationship with a Managing General Underwriter, a benefits consultant simply cannot facilitate the implementation of a true risk management strategy for small business clients."

Managing General Underwriter

A managing general underwriter, as the name implies, performs the actual functions of underwriting and issuing policies. In addition, they have access to the reinsurance marketplace, which is where insurance companies go to buy *their* insurance. Implementing a true risk management strategy, the MGU can extend a reinsurance policy for the (hypothetical, in our example) $280,000–$560,000 deductible exposure and mitigate the risk down to whatever number the employer is comfortable bearing. This provides the employer a fully insured plan with a completely quantified and limited exposure. The analysis then becomes "how much was saved in premium versus how much was paid out in reinsurance premium."

The following case study (using real numbers from an actual 60-employee technology firm) is illustrative of the types of savings to be derived.

Fixed Expense Analysis

	Premium Total Expense	Reinsurance Total Expense	Fixed Total Costs	Employer Expense	Employee Expense
Current Plan	$232,711	$—	$232,711	$138,488	$94,223
Proposed Design	$172,909	$13,000	$185,909	$94,533	$91,376
Potential Savings $	**$46,802**	**$43,955**	$2,847		
Potential Savings %	20%	**32%**	3%		

Fixed + Variable Expense Analysis

	Fixed Total Costs	Deductible* Max. Exposure	Fixed & Variable Total Costs	Employer Expense	Employee Expense
Current Plan	$232,711	$—	$232,711	$138,488	$94,223
Proposed Design	$185,909	$23,000	$208,909	$117,533	$91,376
Guaranteed Savings $	**$23,802**	**$20,955**	$2,847		
Guaranteed Savings %	10%	**15%**	3%		

*Total deductible exposure of $416,000 is distributed as first $23,000 to employer, balance to reinsurance contract.

159

Through a creative plan redesign coupled with the use of reinsurance to limit the employer's deductible exposure, this employer recognized a potential 32 percent and almost $44,000 savings. The employer's guaranteed savings was at least 15 percent and $21,000, with no decrease in coverage, and a decrease in costs to the *employee* of 3 percent. This strategy, little-known as it may be, is almost uniformly effective in the 20–150-employee firm. The moral of the story? Your small business clients need to find a benefits consultant who will introduce them to large business approaches.

Summary

A health savings account can offer many small business owners an attractive savings alternative to "traditional" health-care benefits plans. Careful attention must be paid, however, to the controlling IRS and DOL regulations. Attempting to get too creative with HSA plan design may land an employer in hot water. Beyond the HSA solution, even more creative benefits designs may offer your clients significant savings with little or no reduction in benefits.

Profound Insight #13

The CEO of a large managed care corporation was sitting in his office late one night, gloating about record profits. Suddenly, with an acrid puff of smoke and the smell of brimstone, Satan appeared before him.

Satan smiled at the CEO and said, "I have a proposition for you. You can win every health-care contract you bid on, for the rest of your life. Your colleagues will stand in awe of you, physicians will fear you, and you will make embarrassing sums of money. All I want in exchange is your soul, and the souls of all your friends and the souls of all the shareholders in your company."

The CEO thought about this for a moment, then asked, "So, what's the catch?"

CHAPTER 14

College Funding Strategies and Solutions

The third man in the ring makes boxing possible.

—*Joyce Carol Oates*

The Traditional Approach

When assisting your clients in developing a college savings plan in the past, you may have had good intentions, but in the approach there were some flaws. However, you probably were not 100 percent wrong. Let us look at the traditional planning process and how it will cost substantial dollars that could otherwise be utilized in funding the student's education.

Step 1: How Much Money Will You Need?

Your clients have finally decided to set up a college fund for their son, little Marc, who is five years old. They seek the help of their trusted CPA and financial advisor. We will call him CPA Lance. The first calculation CPA Lance makes is to find out how much money you will need to send little Marc through a four-year college program. CPA Lance is told that the clients would like to pay for 100 percent of Marc's four-year education at an average private school. CPA Lance takes this information and performs the calculations shown in Exhibit 14.1.

Exhibit 14.1   Initial Cost Estimate

Number of years until attending college:	13
Number of years attending college:	4
Today's approximate annual cost:	$26,000
Average annual college inflation rate:	4%
Year	**Annual Cost**
13	$49,027
14	51,478
15	54,052
16	56,755
Total	**$211,312**

Exhibit 14.1 represents the annual and total college cost for Johnny. The inflation percentage, however, is incorrect. CPA Lance used a rate of 4 percent based on the Consumer Price Index. The actual college inflation rate could be as high as 8.4 percent. Let us adjust, in Exhibit 14.2, the calculation and get a more realistic savings target amount.

Exhibit 14.2 illustrates more accurate college savings goals.

CPA Lance has the right idea up to this point. He simply underestimated the college inflation rate, but in doing so, he has underfunded the education goal by more than one third. You may be thinking, "No big deal. The inflation rate may not continue to grow at 8.4 percent in the future." That thought is

Exhibit 14.2   Realistic Cost Estimate

Year	Annual Cost
13	$74,191
14	80,424
15	87,179
16	94,502
Total	**$336,296**

true; however, when estimating future needs, actual historical data should be used in projecting a more likely outcome. The real question is whether you would rather be overfunded for your son's college tuition or have a shortfall that will only carry him through 2½ to 3 years of schooling.

Now that CPA Lance has been informed of the correct inflation number, he tells you that you must plan on a savings program that provides you with $336,296.

Step 2: How Much Money Will You Have to Save?

For this calculation, CPA Lance makes the following assumptions:

After-tax rate of return on investment:	8%
Number of years until the start of college (when funding needs to be complete):	13

CPA Lance indicates that his client must save $1,232.21 per month for the next 13 years. After your client lifts himself off the floor and regains his senses, he pleads with you to come up with some other alternatives. CPA Lance empathizes with you and says there is another way. Instead of funding to the beginning of college, you can fund through the four years of college, thereby giving you extra time to meet this goal. The new calculation reveals the client needs to put aside $1,028.93 per month for 16 full years.

Step 3: What Type of Investment Program Should Be Utilized?

CPA Lance comes back with a proposal to deposit $1,028.93 monthly into two or three mutual funds, with 60 percent of the investment allocated into a U.S. stock growth fund, 25 percent into a balanced mutual fund, and 15 percent into an international stock mutual fund. Lance reviews the prospectus of each fund and highlights past investment results. CPA Lance cautions you that there are no guarantees of future performance, and past performance is not an indication of future returns. By taking some risk on your investments, you may have the ability to reap a higher rate of return. After all, your goal is to achieve 8 percent after tax. Bravo, CPA Lance. A job well done indeed!

Step 4: Who Should Own the Investment Program?

CPA Lance has saved the best for last. He sits fully erect with his chest thrust forward and announces, "Of course you want to have little Johnny own this under a UGMA (Uniform Gift to Minors Act) account." (In some states this is synonymous with a UTMA—Uniform Transfer to Minors Act.) Lance leans closer to you and excitedly says, "By setting this up as a UGMA, you will save substantial taxes on the investment gains by shifting them from your higher tax bracket to Johnny's virtually nonexistent tax bracket. You now have not only a solid education funding program for little Johnny, but at the same time you've got a ter- rific tax-sheltered investment plan." CPA Lance, seemingly euphoric at this point asks, "Doesn't this make all the sense in the world to you?" Your client replies, "CPA Lance, this is even better than I could have possibly hoped for." CPA Lance directs the client to an investment advisor to fill out the necessary paperwork, and your client gives him the first monthly deposit.

The plan is implemented, and your client feels great. He has just started the journey to secure little Johnny's college education.

Good Intentions, Disastrous Consequences

CPA Lance did an excellent job up until Step #4. The owner- ship of the investment program should not be in your child's name under a UGMA account for the following reasons:

During the child's minor years, the parent is the custodian of the account and may make the decision to use the funds in the investment for the benefit of the child. Once the child attains majority (defined by various states as either age 18 or age 21), the parent relinquishes total control of the funds. The child can then use the funds for whatever purpose he or she sees fit. Herein lies the dilemma. If little Johnny does not go to college or perhaps drops out of college, the hard-earned dollars may be utilized for the higher and nobler purpose of social mobility (namely the fastest, shiniest, newest automobile). And, legally, you cannot do a thing about it. With the UGMA, you lose control!

Under a UGMA account for 2007, if the child is under age 18, the first $850 of investment income is tax-free and the next $850 is taxed at the child's rate (presumably at 15 percent, which should be lower than that of the child's parents). All earnings above $1,700 are taxed at the parents' tax rate. Assuming the parents are in a 28 percent tax bracket, that is an annual tax savings on the first $1,700 of investment income of $348.50 per year. Although it is nothing to sneeze at, there are better alternatives. As parents, keep the investment plan in your name.

Current financial aid qualification rules severely penalize any assets owned by the college-bound student. Assets owned by the student lose 35 percent in potential financial aid. Financial aid includes grants and scholarships that are tax-free funds.

I will give you an example to illustrate how devastating this can be. Suppose your client has built up $100,000 in a UGMA account for his child. Your client applies for financial aid, he receives his award letter, and it states that you and your child's ability to pay tuition exceed the annual tuition costs. The primary reason is that the $100,000 in the UGMA will cost you $35,000 per year in potential financial aid. And since this $35,000 is tax-free, that equates to a loss to parents in a 28

167

percent tax bracket of $48,611 in annual earnings to replace the potential financial award. The total loss over four years is $194,444. The extent of loss can be reduced to approximately 12 percent rather than 35 percent by having the parents own the mutual funds. These assets discussed are governed by the current financial formulas and could be subject to change in the future.

Traditional Vehicles

Let us examine several traditional investment vehicles for saving for your client's student's college tuition. Specifically, we address the positive and negative attributes inherent in each of the following:

- Home Equity Loans
- Stocks, Bonds and/or Mutual Funds
- Retirement Plans
- Life Insurance
- Borrowing
- Prepaid Tuition Plans
- Coverdell Educational Savings Account
- IRC Section 529 Plans

Home Equity Loans

Certainly, an option available to any caring parent is to secure a loan in order to pay their student's college tuition and use their home equity as collateral. Needless to say, banks and other financial institutions market these types of programs heavily. These programs are attractive to financial institutions because the home asset is usually one of the most precious assets any family can have. Plus, the ability to repossess the house and sell it in order to pay back a delinquent loan is an excellent source of comfort for the lenders. Additionally, the propensity for homeowners to pay home equity loans rather than lose their homes makes these extremely profitable loans with a minimal occurrence of defaults.

Stocks, Bonds, Mutual Funds

Another popular investment that parents gravitate toward is securities in the form of stocks or bonds, or stock or bond mutual funds. Generally speaking, a parent will begin purchasing equities (stocks or stock mutual funds) or fixed-income securities (bonds, bond mutual funds, money market accounts, and the like) either at a child's early age or as soon as their budget allows such an activity. When the funds are needed for college, parents can each gift to the child up to a maximum of $12,000 in mutual fund shares. By gifting the shares to the child, they can be redeemed in the child's name and that gain will be taxed at the child's tax rate if not subjected to the kiddie tax.

Retirement Plans

Utilizing a 401(k) profit sharing program or some other appropriate retirement plan to save for your student's college education is actually an outstanding idea! Let us examine why this is the case. First and foremost, the contributions you are making to the retirement plan or that are being made by your employer are not only tax deductible on the way in and not taxable to you in the case of the employer making them, but also the investment income that you generate (interest, dividends, capital gains, and the like) is tax deferred until such time as you withdraw it.

Therefore, instead of giving up one third or one half of the investment income you use each year, thereby rendering it useless to make more money for your client, those dollars that would normally go to the government remain in their account and work for them! In this way, they now have personal experience with the magic of compounding interest or compounding rates of return. When utilizing this loan strategy, the absolute necessity is to ensure that their plan has a loan provision. And remember that they will have to repay the loan within five years with interest. If they do not, it is all taxed as current income, and penalties will be assessed.

Life Insurance

Some parents choose to purchase life insurance policies in order to fund for college. Again, this is an example of an outstanding method because it combines tax-deferred investment growth, flexibility, liquidity, and a self-completing feature in the event of death and disability. Let us examine each of these points.

A life insurance contract can be constructed in such a way that it is actually an annuity plan in disguise. Although federal law changes in the 1980s took away some of the attractiveness of this tactic, the major attributes of this program still remain in place. By constructing a life insurance contract so that the maximum portion of the premium is going to a cash value or so-called "inside buildup" and the death benefit is minimized to the level that you would need in order to completely finance your student's education, this allows for an exciting investment. You are able to assure the client's student's education in the event of your client's premature death through the tax-free death benefits featured in virtually all life insurance contracts.

Hopefully your clients will not die prematurely, but instead will be able to access the cash value that has accumulated over the years. These accumulations are available to them tax-free when you surrender or take a distribution from their policy equal to the amount of premiums that have been paid. The gain they have experienced on the policy can normally be borrowed from the contract at attractive interest rates (generally a net rate of 1 percent or 2 percent, depending on the policy). Additionally, your clients can choose different types of investments within these policies. If they are extremely conservative in nature, they could opt for a policy with investments that are basically fixed-income instruments paying interest, or, in the case of a whole life contract, dividends. By borrowing these investment gains, taxation is escaped and, most importantly, the presence of a high cash value life insurance contract on their balance sheet when you apply for financial aid is simply a nonevent.

Effectively, the financial aid people do not count this as an asset when calculating your ability to pay. Disclaimer: Single pay life insurance is treated as an investment by most private institutions and by the IRS. It is important that you make your insurance person aware of what you are trying to accomplish. If you follow these guidelines, cash buildup is exempt from the financial aid formulas. Therefore, you enjoy tax-free growth of the investment along with the self-completing feature for death. Again, this is one of the absolute best ways to save for college.

If a parent, or any relative, uses life insurance as part of their savings program they need to be careful. There are many insurance companies, and some offer better products than others. Experience indicates that you may want to utilize a low- or no-load product. You also want to have the insurance underwritten (issued) with the best possible rating. Someone skilled with experience would be the best place to go for assistance. You may want to consult someone with a CLU (Chartered Life Underwriter) or a PFS (Personal Financial Specialist) designation for assistance.

Another thing to consider is for whom the insurance is issued. As an example, consider a situation in which a large policy is being purchased by a father to be used for college saving. It was discovered, before the insurance was applied for, that there would be medical underwriting problems with the father. He had various medical problems. If the insurance was applied for, there would be a permanent record with the medical information bureau. The insurance company that the insurance salesperson was recommending was not highly rated, the product was probably unsuitable for the person's risk tolerance and the commission was huge. The CPA had recommended the insurance salesperson. The salesperson was new in the insurance business. After discussions with the CPA, it was recommended that the insurance be purchased on the wife, who would probably be issued insurance in the preferred category. Since the parents were conservative with their money, a more suitable insurance product was selected. Applications were submitted to a few low- and no-load insurance companies on a trial application. If a medical problem was discovered, there would be no medical information bureau record for the person. The father already had a substantial amount of life insurance, in the preferred nonsmoker category. Had he applied for life insurance, he would have been heavily rated (charged a lot more money due to poor health). The insurance salesperson had already started canceling this person's perfectly good existing life insurance.

Even though the CPA was not going to receive a commission, the CPA was not helping the client in this situation. The wife had no insurance and had a good job. The husband had a large amount of life insurance. Shortly after the wife obtained her insurance, in the preferred category, the life insurance salesperson left the life insurance business. Another service that insurance professionals should provide is continuing service.

Borrowing

Next, we come to another traditional method of funding college. This method is effective, yet not creative, and is fraught with pitfalls. It is basic, good old-fashioned borrowing. Earlier we discussed the pros and cons of utilizing a home equity loan. Personal loans can be even more disadvantageous because they generally command higher origination fees, upfront prepaid interest (in the form of points), collateral (in the event that they are secured), or higher interest rates (in the event that it is an unsecured personal loan). The same drawbacks that apply to a home equity loan apply to this type of loan because you or your student still has to repay the loan. The interest expense is not deductible because it is a personal or consumer loan; therefore, the amount paid back to the financial institution is generally much more than the amount borrowed. This either reduces the level of comfort in your retirement years or increases the debt burden on your client's student, hitting them pretty close to the time they receive their diploma. This should be a last resort method and is generally only pursued by those who fail to plan at an early enough stage.

When put into a position where borrowing becomes a necessity, the parent should look to those loan programs that are sponsored by the federal government: the Stafford and the PLUS loans.

The Stafford Loan is a student loan with specific limits: $3,500 for a first year student, $4,500 for a sophomore, and $5,500 for juniors and seniors. Provided it is a subsidized loan, there will be no interest charges and no required payments while the student is in college or during the deferment period. Once the student has graduated and the deferment has lapsed, payments must commence.

The PLUS loan is a parental loan. Payments need to made within 30 days of the loan dispersal to the college. The normal repayment period is 10 years, but this can be extended if there are multiple debts and may be combined into one monthly payment. The Stafford Loan and the PLUS Loan carry life and disability insurance that covers the borrower and the student. In the event of either occurrence, the debt is cancelled.

Prepaid Tuition Plans

These are programs that allow the parent to prepay their future student's education. Typically, the plan allows the parent to purchase bonds within a state-run trust that is tax-exempt. This contract guarantees a future education at current costs. Here is how it works. If the cost of the college is presently $20,000 and you invest in a $10,000 contract, you have locked in 50 percent of the cost of that school. When it is time to redeem the contract, assuming that the cost of college has risen to $30,000, your contract will be worth $15,000. If it has risen to $36,000, it will be worth $18,000. With these prepayment plans, you are locking in your future cost at present values. Keep in mind that, over recent history, the increases in the cost of education have far outpaced the rate of inflation, so this may not be a bad idea.

What are the disadvantages of prepayment? Some states only provide this service for their own state-run institutions. What if your student decides to go to a private school, or out of your state of residence, or not at all? Typically, you will receive your principal back, but it may not be adjusted for inflation. I know of no state that will allow you to participate in the appreciation of the investment under the above circumstances. Read over these plans carefully.

Coverdell Savings Account

Beginning in the year 2002, Congress has allowed taxpayers the ability to contribute $2,000 (per beneficiary) into a tax-favored educational individual retirement account. Previously, the limit was $500. Although greatly expanded, this will fall far short for most individuals considering the current expense of college funding. Multiple contracts are permitted for a single beneficiary but may not exceed the $2,000 limit in any one taxable year. Any excess contributions are subject to a 6 percent penalty annually as long as the extra funds remain in the account.

All contributions are permitted to grow tax-deferred and, if used to pay for qualified educational expenses, will come out tax-free. The contribution is treated as a nontaxable gift to the beneficiary and there is no tax deduction permitted for the gift by the contributor. There are no limits to the number of beneficiaries that one contributor can set up and the contributor does not have to be related to the beneficiary.

IRC Section 529 Plans

How about a disclaimer on the front end? IRC Section 529 Plans are state sponsored and, though they must adhere to specific IRC guidelines, the individual intricacies will vary widely. It is far beyond the scope of this chapter to cover each and every state. For specific information on each state's plan, go to www.savingforcollege.com. This site has links to each state-sponsored plan. When considering one of these state-sponsored plans, the individual should pay close attention to who manages the account, how many investment choices there are, past performance, expenses, annual fees and, if so, how much, whether UGMA or UTMA accounts can be transferred into the plan, and whether your own state plan yields a state tax deduction and, if so, what the cap on that deduction is. There is no federal tax deduction allowed for any plan.

In general, the 529 plan is a vehicle to save for college. The plans are state sponsored and are managed by mutual funds and insurance companies. Neither the account owner nor the beneficiary is allowed to directly manage the account. The owner is allowed to decide among several investment strategies based on his own risk tolerance and time horizon. If the beneficiary is young, he may opt for a 100 percent equity position; if older, more of a balance among equities, bonds, and cash. If the beneficiary is close to the time that disbursements will be needed to fund his or her education, the owner may take a more conservative stance and move away from equities altogether and place the money into bonds and money markets.

The amount of the contribution for each taxable year is limited to the gift tax exclusion, currently $12,000. There is one exception to this rule. A single individual may gift $60,000 to a single beneficiary in one year, provided that no further contributions are made for the next five taxable years. Married couples may split gifts to a single beneficiary and contribute up to $120,000 in one taxable year. This is often used as an estate-planning tool. Once the gift is made, the IRS considers this a completed gift, and the amount of the gift is excluded from the individual's estate. Multiple beneficiaries may be chosen, so you can see that, with a large family, it would not take long to shelter large sums of money from current estate taxes. Contributions must be made in cash. Several factors, such as age of the beneficiary, current costs, inflation, and expected investment returns limit the maximum contribution to a single beneficiary. These maximums have already been determined by each state. Experience has shown that these plans vary from $170,000 to nearly $300,000. As stated earlier, contributions are not tax deductible but will grow tax-deferred. If the assets are used for qualified expenses, they will come out tax-free.

Two things must be considered when adopting these plans. These plans came about in 2001 under EGTRRA (Economic Growth Tax Relief Reconciliation Act) and unless EGTRRA is extended, they will expire in 2010. Second, it is unclear at this time if all states will consider this a completed gift when it comes to eligibility for Medicaid. Investment returns on these plans may vary from state to state. You should discuss this matter with local counsel, as well as its effect on the overall client plan.

I am sure you can perceive that you want to structure your investment portfolio in such a way that certain goals are achieved.

When at all possible, look for tax leveraging on the investment vehicle selected. Simply stated, seek a tax deduction from the funding vehicle on the way in (generally most readily available in qualified retirement plans), and look for as many tax-deferred attributes to the investment as are possible (generally present with life insurance and annuity contracts). Select those investments that are not considered an asset for purposes of calculating your expected family contribution. Those types of investments tend to be annuities, life insurance contracts, and assets in a qualified retirement plan. Be sure your retirement plan has a loan provision, and carefully study that provision to see if it involves restrictions in any way through a vesting schedule (that schedule of time that you have to be a participant in the plan before you can access any or all of the money), or any restrictions or prohibitions on the funding aspects of the program.

Because of the severe consequences that could result, including their aid-reducing qualities, avoid investments of any nature that end up in your student's name. As previously explained, your financial aid that is otherwise available will be reduced by $0.35 for every dollar your student has saved.

Avoid those investments that require you to pay between one quarter and one half of your investment gains to the government. This is extremely adverse to the whole idea of saving for college education, because you are trying to accumulate wealth and here the government is reducing your wealth through taxes.

Look to control the assets by keeping them in your name versus the student's name. Now, I may be striking a chord, because you know your client's son or daughter would never do anything with those dollars that they worked so hard to accumulate for them except what they want them to do with them. I would like to believe that this is true in all cases, but I would be an irresponsible advisor if I did not at least point out the potential that the money could be spent on something that they would rather it not be. I think I will leave it at that and let you deal with your client's emotions and ideas on this subject rather than beat this point to death.

Finally, we live in an uncertain world; therefore, if you are going to plan for your client's student's education, you need to manage all the risks that are involved. No matter how excellent their health may be, there is a risk of their premature death. There's also the possibility that they may be unable to work as a result of a disability. Therefore, please consider strongly insuring against the two biggest perils that will derail their plan. Simply stated, manage the risk of premature death by insuring the value of their lives, and purchase a life insurance contract. Also, since they probably insure their home or apartment, automobile, and other objects that they value, why not insure their own little personal moneymaking machine? Their own personal moneymaking machine is their ability to engage in productive work and generate income.

How do you insure such a machine? Purchase a disability insurance plan or at least be sure that you coordinate both life insurance and disability insurance at your place of employment. They may be fortunate enough to work in an organization that provides these benefits; however, for many reasons beyond the scope of this text, they seldom are adequate for this type of single-purpose risk management effort. However, they should be considered when you ultimately calculate how much of these programs you might otherwise need.

Clients should never be put into a position where they have saved themselves $3,000 in college costs and find they have increased their tax burden by $6,000. Remember that financial aid and the tax laws do not walk the same path. Before implementing any plan, the CPA and client should sit down and review the plan together. You are paying these professionals to advise you. Your CPA is part of your team, so do not hesitate to put him in the lineup.

Owning a business gives one a great deal of flexibility as opposed to those who rely on W-2 income. For instance, take the value of an asset that is in the individual's name. The entire value of this asset can be included in the formula. But if this asset were placed in a business, the value would be adjusted down 40 percent of that value up to the first $80,000. As the owner of a C corporation, you have the ability to control your own income. Being able to regulate that income provides you with the opportunity to control your adjusted gross income, which is one of the factors in determining your expected family contribution.

Hey, Mr. or Ms. Businessperson, what about putting the student to work? This would create a deductible expense in your business. The student is paying income taxes at a lesser rate, may be eligible for a lesser FICA tax, and will be contributing to their quest for their own education. Not a bad deal for all. You have created a deductible tuition expense, but keep in mind that you must follow a couple of guidelines: (1) the student must perform meaningful services, and (2) the payment made must be reasonable for the service performed.

So, what is exempt from the view of these all-encompassing formulas, either Congressional or institutional? Well, quite frankly, not much. The following list shows exempt assets, which are listed on the FAFSA (Free Application for Federal Student Aid) and the Profile financial aid application forms.

- Retirement plans
- Pension funds

- Annuities
- IRAs
- Keogh plans
- Life insurance policies (single premium insurance policies are considered an investment and are therefore not exempt)
- Your home, if it is your principal residence (FAFSA only)
- Your farm, if it is your principal residence and you file a schedule F with your tax return (FAFSA only)

As you review all of these traditional approaches, you can choose to either agree or disagree with me. I also do not want to finish this discussion without stating that any method you use to save money to provide for your future or the future of your child is an excellent method, because you are doing something. However, because we live in an uncertain time and we have to deal with issues like death, taxes, and disability, there are some investments and some saving techniques that are better than others.

Real Life

In this section we look at the actual cases of a few of my past clients. Changes have been made to some of the circumstances and names in order to protect their privacy. We also review situations of varying incomes and assets. We look at where they were prior to taking charge of their circumstances and where they ended up after going through the process.

Time for a disclaimer. Remember that everyone's situation is unique. I am not suggesting that if you follow one of these scenarios, then you are going to get a great award letter. They are only intended to demonstrate what worked in one client's particular situation. I encourage you to research the process, talk to the universities to find out what guidelines they will be using, and find a financial advisor who is totally familiar with the financial aid system and your individual needs. Then and only then should you develop a plan and implement it. Keep in mind that in any good plan you must prepare for three possible events. One, things could get worse. Two, things could get better. And three, things could stay the same. Your plan should take all of these possibilities into account and offer you the flexibility to adjust to any of the above scenarios. Never lock yourself into any plan that does not offer you some back doors. What if your client's son or daughter decides to head into the military or take a few years off before deciding on a college, or selects a college that is not so well endowed? No matter how good your plan is, if the college has no money to help, all is for naught. Or what if your client's son or daughter decides that they are not going to college at all? Where is their back door then?

If your client is like most of us, probably the biggest asset your client presently owns is the equity in his home. Be careful when evaluating its present market worth. When completing the FAFSA this is not a concern, because you are not asked this question, but it will be asked with respect to other real property that you may own.

In the Profiles instruction book, you are told not to use the appraised value, the insured value, or the tax value, so what is left? They ask for what you could expect to receive if you were to sell your home today. Fair market value. What is this? For those who were caught up in the real estate market of recent years you can understand how arbitrary this statement is. Many a client comes in and finds that they owe more than the appraised value of the property. Consider this: The formula does not accommodate negative values, so there is no offset to a positive asset. So how do you determine fair market value in a market economy that has such ups and downs?

The colleges and universities look at several factors in determining the minimum value that they will accept, hence the term minimum derived value. First they look at the year you purchased your property and then at the purchase price. Now they multiply this figure by a factor that attaches an appreciation rate to come up with present value. The colleges use this as a guideline and it is at their discretion to adjust it up or down. Most of the colleges will accept any valuation that is above this minimum value. This is not a substitute for the fair market value, which should be included on the form, but when it becomes difficult to determine the worth in this present real estate market, it is an acceptable guideline.

With this information in mind and to give you a more practical approach to this process, I have asked a long-time associate to share some of his past experiences working with his clients. Richard Preston has been in the college planning arena for the past 14 years and has authored a book titled *Intuition,* which was published in 1996.

Situation 1

In this situation, we discuss a widower with an annual income of approximately $200,000. He owned his home, had a small mortgage on it, and had more than $300,000 in stocks and mutual funds. He had three children in college, and his daughter planned to start college in the fall. Her selection of colleges included Yale and Harvard.

The father had never qualified for financial aid. We were also looking down the road to providing a college education for four more children. Even with the growth potential and liquidity of his investments and the equity in his home, it would not be enough to cover the price tag that he would face to educate his children. His biggest asset was his ability to generate substantial income, without which none of this would be possible.

Given his circumstances, his expected family contribution, before any changes were to be made, was $29,584. Needless to say, he did not qualify for any aid.

182

Problems

- To provide a college education to all the children.
- To maintain some degree of liquidity.
- To ensure, in the event of disability or death, that the plan would be self-completing.
- To provide some asset protection so that he would not be put into a position where he could not start saving for retirement until too late an age.

Recommendations

- Sell the securities.
- Increase the mortgage on the home.
- Purchase a single pay immediate annuity to feed a high cash-value life insurance contract.
- Purchase a second annuity that would return a monthly income to help defray some of the monthly expenses.

Rationale

- By following the above recommendations, we would lower the EFC to $10,832 and put them in a position to receive aid.
- By using the annuity and the high cash-value life insurance, we would change a nonexempt asset into an exempt asset.
- The father would have access to the cash buildup in the contract, either through policy loans or direct withdrawals.
- We would ensure that, in the event of his death, there would be money available for college expense.
- The disability rider would ensure that if anything were to happen to disable the father, the contract would be self-completing. The insurance company, with this type of rider,

is obligated to make all premium payments for the life of the contract.

- We would provide monthly payments to help with the cash flow, while the asset itself would be exempt from the formula.
- If our plan were to work and we found a college that could meet the need for financial aid, the money in the insurance contract would be available for retirement.

Results

- In the following year, the total of all the awards for his three children in college totaled $31,438.
- We will be preparing for his son to enter college this fall.

Situation 2

In this case, we have a small business owner who runs his business as a sole proprietorship, which he valued at $225,000. His wife worked as a bookkeeper and draws a minimum salary to qualify for Social Security benefits. They were a family of five, their adjusted gross income was $82,860 per year, they had approximately $35,000 of securities, and a second home that they rented during the summer, which generated $500 per month. A sale of a separate business, which was pending, was going to generate $65,000 within the next year. Their home may have been overvalued because of its location and the inflated prices of coastal properties during the late 1990s. The husband had $200,000 of term insurance on himself with a $50,000 rider on his wife.

Their daughter was a sophomore in high school. She was a good student with the potential of getting aid if the family could qualify. Based on their current circumstances, the expected family contribution was $23,770.

Problems

- To provide an education to all children without eating up all the assets.
- To ensure that, in the event of any unexpected circumstances, money could be available if needed.
- To ensure that, in the event of disability or death of one of the primary wage earners, the plan could self-complete.
- To plan for the retirements of the parents, so that when college was not an issue, they would not have gone through all their assets and in later years have to plan for retirement all over again.
- To lessen the impact of the business as it relates to the formulas.
- To provide a vehicle so that the money generated from the sale of the separate business would not hurt them. This was part of their retirement.
- The family was facing approximately $350,000 in educational costs.

Recommendations

- Sell the securities being held.
- With the proceeds of selling the stock, start a variable annuity.
- From the sale of the separate business, start a single-pay immediate annuity that would feed a life policy.
- Purchase a high cash-value life insurance policy on the wife that will be fed from the annuity. This insurance product must have a rider that allows you to dump cash in with your premium payments. Care must be taken so as not to create a modified endowment contract, thereby losing the advantages of a life insurance contract. We will also add a disability rider.
- Revalue the home.

- Revalue the business.
- Include the value of the second property in the business.
- Change the business entity to a C Corporation.
- Lower the business owner's salary.
- Raise his wife's salary.

Rationale

- By following the above recommendations, we would lower the EFC substantially, and put them in a position to receive aid.
- By using the annuity and the high cash-value life insurance, we would change a nonexempt asset into an exempt asset.
- We would give the parents access to the cash buildup in the contract, either through policy loans or direct withdrawals.
- We would ensure that, in the event of the death of either parent, there would be money available for college expense.
- The disability rider would ensure that, if anything were to happen to disable either parent, the contract would be self-completing. The insurance company with this type of rider is obligated to make all premium payments for the life of the contract.
- If our plan were to work, and we found a college that could meet the need for financial aid, the money in the insurance contract would be available for retirement.
- The money from the securities would be placed into a variable annuity that would be exempt from the financial aid formulas.
- The home would be reevaluated to reflect a more current value.
- Because he is the owner of the business, and because without him there would be no business, we could take a

leaner look at the value of that business. If anything were to happen to him, the value of that business would be nothing more than the salvage value that his wife would be able to derive in a forced sale.

- By reclassifying the business as a C Corporation, all profits derived from the business would be taken off the personal tax returns. The C Corporation would be its own entity and file its own tax return. And the business would have the same discounted value that was just indicated above. The first $50,000 of profit in a C Corporation would be taxed at a 15 percent rate rather than at his personal tax rate of 35 percent.
- By lowering the owner's salary and raising his wife's salary, we could take full advantage of the second-to-work credit, which maxes out at about $10,000 of annual salary.

Results

- Their first daughter was accepted at Simmons and received an award letter for more than $20,000.

Summary

Today's practitioner must be aware of a multitude of financial strategies and products to properly serve, retain, and gain clients. Many financial products are being marketed and used incorrectly. The CPA should know the pros and cons of the current strategies being employed by financial professionals in developing comprehensive financial plans for individuals and businesses.

Many clients of CPAs are concerned about college savings. They look to the CPA for guidance. The CPA should be knowledgeable about the various tax efficient ways to save for college.

Profound Insight #14

Don't let this be you:

Actual statement from an insurance claim form:

"I saw a slow-moving, sad-faced old gentleman as he bounced off the roof of my car."

CHAPTER 15

Two Alternative Investments for Financial Independence

He who is not courageous enough to take risks will accomplish nothing in life.

—*Muhammad Ali*

The bulk of this book has been devoted to advising you on how to help your clients avoid being "ripped off," but we would be remiss if we did not at least proffer one or two suggestions on how best to advise your clients to recoup some of their hard-earned money lost in the (stock and/or real estate) market. What good is knowing how to avoid losing money, after all, when you've already lost it, and have no way to get it back?

Let us start with a relatively unknown investment that has arguably the single most favorable risk/reward ratio of any product available to the retail client. You recall that Chapter 12 was spent describing various aspects of the relatively little known secondary market for life insurance policies, the life settlement market. Interestingly, what happens to a policy after it is sold into the secondary marketplace is both a legitimate and exceedingly rewarding question.

The Tertiary Market

Broadly speaking, the vast majority of life insurance policies sold into the secondary market are purchased by intermediaries using institutional capital. Generally, most of these are bundled, securitized, and resold as blocks of business to large institutional investors. (Warren Buffet's Berkshire Hathaway is a large and often-cited investor in life settlements.) A limited number of life settlement purchasers has taken a somewhat different approach, however—the resale of policies obtained via the secondary marketplace to individual investors. Most often, these resales take the form of "fractional interests" in the available policies. A given investor purchases *X percent* of a particular policy, and the investor's rate of return is wholly dependent on the life span of the insured.

The United States Court of Appeals, For The District Of Columbia Circuit (1996) No. 95–5364 *Securities and Exchange Commission, Appellee v. Life Partners, Incorporated And Brian D. Pardo, Appellants Consolidated with 96–5018, 96–5090* examined whether fractional interests are securities. Inasmuch as

> *The final requirement of the Howey test for an investment to be deemed a security is that the profits expected by the investor be derived from the efforts of others.*

was not satisfied, the fractional interests offered by Life Partners Inc. (LPI) were deemed *not* to be securities. Whether this finding can be generally applied to the offering of fractional interests in life settlements by other vendors remains an open question. This relatively narrow ruling holds, for the time being, in the State of Texas, but that has not prevented other states (Colorado, Virginia, etc.) from bringing suit against purveyors of fractional life settlements for purported violations of regulatory schema.

What *must* be emphasized is, so far to the best of our knowledge, that *no* retail investor in life settlements has filed a claim pursuant to a failure on the part of LPI (or any of their various competitors) to "pay off" in a timely fashion, upon policy maturity. The consumer remains overwhelmingly satisfied with the structure and return of these investments, as evidenced by a remarkably high (claimed >85 percent) reinvestment rate among purchasers. To date, LPI remains a publicly traded company, engaged in both the purchase of life insurance policies and the resale of fractional interests in those policies (with claimed annual returns of 12.9 percent over the past 14 years) to individual investors. Institutional investors such as pension funds and insurance companies remain the largest purchasers in what has become recognized as the tertiary market.

History

Flash backward to the 1980s. In the early (untreatable) stages of the AIDS epidemic, relatively large numbers of formerly healthy life insurance policyholders were looking at an early death sentence. A cottage industry arose in which speculators (some called them "vultures") would purchase, at considerable discount from face value, the life insurance policies of the victims—many of whom utilized the proceeds from the sale of their policies to pay for medical treatment. The almost wholly unregulated nature of these transactions, coupled with the frankly unethical behavior and seemingly opportunistic motives of many of the purchasers, combined to taint the industry as it stood. As an aside, the purchase of a life insurance policy in which the insured has been underwritten and deemed to have a life expectancy of less than two years (as was the case with most of the AIDS victims in the 1980s) is now most commonly referred to as a viatical settlement, and the proceeds are potentially subject to different (long-term capital gains) tax treatment than those from a life settlement.

Over the course of the next few decades, the life settlements industry matured considerably. The speculators looking to make a quick buck off the backs of the terminally ill have been more or less relegated to the dark corners of the marketplace, and comprise a relatively small percentage (one industry expert quoted a figure of less than 15 percent) of current transactions. Gradually, the industry has evolved into a secondary market for policies that are of considerable benefit to consumers. As stated by Wharton financial experts Doherty & Singer in *The Benefits of a Secondary Market for Life Insurance Policies (2002),*

> *The magnitude of the benefits is positively correlated to the quantity of coverage sold to life settlement firms and to the improvement in the terms of accelerated death benefits offered by incumbent carriers. We conclude that the incumbent life insurance carriers' efforts to deter entry by life settlement firms are motivated by the anticompetitive desire to maintain monopsony power over policyholders.*

Although the continually developing secondary market is of undeniable benefit to consumers, the equally robust but even less well-known tertiary market has, to date, been limited almost entirely to institutional investors. Curious. Why wouldn't Wall Street want to let the individual investor in on one of its more profitable secrets?

Risk

"Would you be willing to accept commensurately greater risk for the possibility of increased returns over the long term?" How many times have your clients been asked some version of that question? "Everybody knows" that you have to accept more risk in order to get better returns. Well, guess what? Like much

192

of the other baloney that you hear coming from Wall Street, that little bit of conventional wisdom is just that. Baloney!

Consider this. Have you ever heard of a legitimate life insurance company that did not pay an uncontested claim? Insurance companies are compelled by state regulatory agencies to maintain adequate reserves for a reason. They *will* pay a duly-authorized death benefit on a properly maintained policy. The only question is when.

In one respect, fractional life settlement investment can be viewed as akin to the purchase of a zero-coupon bond. An upfront investment of dollar amount X will yield a return of dollar amount Y (and here is where we differ from a zero-coupon bond) at time Z to be determined. There is virtually no risk to principal in a properly maintained policy. The virtual certainty that an investment-grade policy will pay the death benefit makes the risk profile of the contractually determined return only somewhat greater than that of an investment in treasury bills.

Mark Boehm, a life settlements and life insurance advisor, adds a caveat: "One risk unique to the Life Settlements investment is what might be termed 'Longevity Risk'—the possibility that a particular individual, blessed with the Methuselah gene, might live to be 900-plus years old, and drastically reduce the ROI of a particular policy." This risk is mitigated for both institutional and retail investors through the use of independent, third-party actuarial firms, which serve as providers of mortality (life expectancy [LE]) estimates to the insurance industry. The more accurate the life expectancy information, the more precisely the actual return to an investor can be predicted.

Longevity risk is also minimized by virtue of the fact that fractional life settlements purchase price generally includes an escrow amount sufficient to pay the policy premiums well beyond the insured's expected mortality date. As of the date of this writing, Life Partners escrows funds until the predicted endpoint of a two-year LE range, or midpoint plus 12 months.

Competitors to LPI claim an advantage by escrowing the funds for predicted LE plus 24 months, thus theoretically minimizing the possibility of a "premium call"—a request for more funds from existing investors to cover the cost of maintaining the policy in force.

Says Boehm, "Another factor to consider is that these investments are really not at all liquid. The investor must truly be prepared to Buy and Hold. The flip side, of course, is that unlike the stock market, every day the investor holds the investment brings them just a little bit closer to the point when it will pay off."

Reward

Life Partners has paid on thousands of policies at maturity, and investors have realized 12-plus percent returns. Policies offered in the tertiary market are generally priced to provide an anticipated yield in the 12 percent to 15 percent range, with competitors to LPI offering somewhat higher anticipated yields. In comparison to the performance of the stock, bond, or real estate markets over a similar time period, this performance might be accurately characterized as superior.

Coupled with the low relative risk, one can understand why fractional life settlements is a growing, thriving (for the time being), "niche" market. As with other recommendations described here, it is incumbent on the tax advisor to align themselves with an experienced knowledgeable consultant, in order to deliver recommendations appropriate for the client's particular circumstances.

Another Alternative

Profitable business owners might also consider the many benefits associated with direct investment in domestic production of oil and gas. According to Ole Cram, a leading authority on oil and gas (O&G) investments and president of Marcobe Investments Inc., a direct participation in properly structured oil and gas drilling ventures, along with defining and following an appropriate oil and gas investment strategy, will provide:

- Unique tax advantages resulting in lower tax cost
- An alternative income stream from productive oil and gas wells
- A risk mitigation tool to hedge against rising energy and fuel costs

O&G Advantages

Congress has provided unique tax advantages to encourage more production of domestic sources of energy to reduce dependence on foreign sources.

These advantages include:

- Full deduction of investment: 100 percent deduction of invested funds in an oil–gas drilling venture against all income types including business income, salary, portfolio, and capital gains
- Reduction of alternative minimum tax (AMT) income: Up to 40 percent dollar-for-dollar reduction in alternative minimum tax (AMT) income for each invested dollar
- Avoiding AMT: Oil and gas well income will not put you in an AMT situation
- Tax-free income: The first 15 percent to 23 percent of yearly income from the oil–gas well is not taxed due to a depletion allowance, which is similar to how depreciation works in real estate

Working interest in an oil–gas well is not considered a passive activity per IRS Tax Code 469 c.3 Paragraph A so deductions can offset all income from all sources. However, only the indirect drilling costs (IDC) involved with drilling an oil or gas well can be deducted fully the first year.

This usually ranges from 65 percent to 80 percent of the amount invested and includes costs for labor, drilling mud, chemicals, and other items that will not stay with the well when it is put online. The remaining funds cover the tangible drilling costs (TDC)—road improvements, well casing, pump, and other items that stay with the well—and can be deducted as depreciation over seven years until all 100 percent of invested funds are eventually deducted (see IRS Tax Code 263). If the well does not produce any oil or gas (considered a dry hole), then the full investment is deductible the first year.

For those of you who are in an AMT situation, line 25 of IRS form 6251 can be skipped for oil and gas income if you make an election under IRC 59(e) to write off intangible drilling costs over 60 months for regular tax purposes.

Taking your deductions over five years means they do not count as a tax preference item—supporting taking the deduction from AMT income. As long as your IDC deduction does not exceed 40 percent of your AMT income, you can use these deductions. If you are not in an AMT situation, you add back IDC deductions in excess of the 40 percent of your estimated AMT income.

The 1990 Tax Act provided another benefit to investors in the domestic production of oil and gas—tax-free yearly income. Each year a minimum of 15 percent of the income from the well is not taxed due to a depletion allowance. Similar to how depreciation of the building works in real estate investments, there is an understanding that these wells will only produce oil and gas for so many years. This process is termed a depletion allowance that is allowed each year against the resulting income.

For businesses with high energy costs, a properly structured investment strategy for direct investment in oil and gas drilling ventures can provide another income source that will rise as oil and gas prices rise. This strategy usually considers the percentage of revenues used to pay energy costs, the level of risk associated with these investments, and available risk capital to determine an optimized solution for your business.

When considering specific oil and gas ventures, conduct thorough due diligence on the associated company before making an investment. There are many oil and gas investments being touted to investors of which only a few have the expertise and experience to lower the risk of a dry hole. Find other successful investors in oil and gas to learn who they are invested with. Move forward by systematically executing your investment strategy.

Summary

Clients may come to their tax advisor seeking not only tax advice, but advice on how to recoup some of their market losses. It is incumbent on the advisor to recommend those investments that present with a favorable risk–reward profile, in case the advisor himself risks endangering the relationship. Conversely, a recommendation with which both client and advisor are comfortable will perform as predicted will solidify the position as "trusted advisor."

Profound Insight #15

Two stockbrokers (firm believers in "efficient markets") are walking down the street.

One sees a dollar lying on the sidewalk, and says so.

"Obviously not," says the other. "If there were, someone would have picked it up!"

CHAPTER 16

Avoiding Fraud:
Small Business Case Study

You always say, "I'll quit when I start to slide," and then one morning you wake up and realize you done slid.

—*Sugar Ray Robinson*

Introduction

Ann Burch was employed with the J.L. Kirkpatrick Company in Springfield, North Carolina, as a manager of accounts payable. The J.L. Kirkpatrick Company manufactured tools and equipment for the maintenance of yards and gardens. They had achieved steady profitable growth for more than 70 years. Family-owned, the company had been well-managed and many of the employees had long tenure. The company employs about 2,000 people in three locations. Hardware stores, garden centers, and farm suppliers in the Southeast are well-stocked with their tools and accessories. The town of Springfield, population 125,000 is in a farming community in the eastern part of the state.

Ms. Burch was a single parent with two children and a friendly person who sought approval from others. She was primarily responsible for the accounting and payment of company credit cards, the general accounting for two affiliate companies, and accounting for employee expense reimbursements. She had been with the company for six years and was a steady worker who liked to seek out new assignments in other departments. Although she liked to do projects for other departments, some of the assignments were not done well because she did not have the skills and knowledge to do the work she had requested.

Suspicion

In early 2007, I received a phone call from a friend of mine, Tom Bennett, who has a CPA practice in the area. He was a former controller of the company and had left in 2000. He mentioned that the company had contacted him about a special project. The company had become aware of a fraud that had taken place by someone in the accounting department. Tom did not have the time for the project because of the imminent start of tax season. Tom mentioned my name to Bill Thompson, Vice-President of Human Resources, as someone he knew was trustworthy and could do the work. The length of the project was unknown but the CFO estimated it would take at least two to three weeks. Tom said if I was interested to contact the Bill Thompson.

I called Bill the next day and discussed the assignment that he said would involve reviewing invoices, travel expense vouchers, and copies of cancelled checks. We discussed my professional experience of 30 years in the controller's function with several companies. Mr. Thompson said he would talk with the chief financial officer, George Edwards, and that I would hear from him. The next day Mr. Edwards called and discussed the assignment with me. We arranged to meet on a Friday afternoon.

In the meeting with Mr. Edwards, I learned that he had been with the company about 15 months. He noted early in

the conversation that "the internal controls are very lax here"
For example, there was not enough segregation of duties in
the accounting manager's position. The manager, Ms. Burch,
received the company credit card statements, recorded the
accounting entries, and approved the monthly payments to the
credit card companies. She was the custodian of the credit cards
as well.

Investigation

The investigation commenced the following Tuesday, January
23, 2007, as I began reviewing invoices from a vendor's file
where checks were found payable to Ms. Burch's personal
credit card companies. According to the IT department's help
desk technician, Ms. Burch made requests to change the payee
on the accounting records to a legitimate vendor's name to
cover up for the actual payee of the check that went to her
credit card company. Additional information about her own
personal credit cards was found on the hard drive of her com-
puter in her office. An analysis of the hard drive was done by
a security consulting firm, Jacobs and Lassiter, which was hired
by the J.L. Kirkpatrick Company.

The company hired this firm to review the documentation
prepared in the case, interview some of the employees, and
work with the outside legal counsel. The security firm had
extensive experience working with law enforcement and the
district attorney's office. After the interviews, the CFO and the
investigator concluded there were no other employees involved
with Ms. Burch in the schemes to defraud the company. Also
assisting the company was their law firm, Drake and Williams.

The documentation prepared by the CFO, director of
accounting, and myself would be used in the claim to be filed
under their insurance policy. An FBI agent was brought in to
assist in the case at the request of the district attorney. I met

with him in March 2007 at the company's request, to review and explain the documentation to him.

Fraud

Ann Burch also had responsibility for the accounting and monthly payment of company-issued credit cards. She used some of the cards for her own personal expenses. She also applied for a credit card from the same bank in the name of the company and used it only for her personal expenses to support a lavish lifestyle. She purchased merchandise online and sold the items to other people, including company employees, to raise cash for her own use.

Total fraudulent transactions from all the company credit cards exceeded $57,000. Ms. Burch told fellow employees that she had come into an inheritance from an aunt who passed away. Examination of the company's file copies of monthly credit card statements showed some expenses with no receipts. Also, some of the transactions were lined out in black ink by Ms. Burch, but you could still see the vendor's name when held up to a light.

Another fraud committed by Ms. Burch was the creation of checks using employees' names for expense reimbursements and petty cash replenishment. The endorsements were forged by her and the checks were enclosed in an envelope and delivered to the company's treasurer's department to go into the daily bank deposit bag. Instructions with the envelope were for the bank to cash the checks and the cash was delivered back to Ann Burch for supposed delivery to the respective employees; however, she would pocket the cash. Examination of several travel expense reimbursements showed they were for even amounts, which are unusual for this type expense, and the endorsements were not similar to the respective employee's authentic signature. In fact, the endorsements were similar to Ms. Burch's signature. The fraud ($30,000) went undetected for several years through false general ledger entries and poor internal accounting controls.

There are two affiliate companies, Shelby Exports in Biloxi, Mississippi, and Hertford Supply Company in Tucson, Arizona. Ann Burch had responsibility for issuing disbursements, reconciling the bank accounts, and maintaining the general ledgers for these two companies. For Shelby Exports, she would create fraudulent checks for nonexistent vendors. The payments and checks were printed in her office and delivered by the company's courier service to the local bank to be cashed and monies delivered to Ms. Burch. Copies of the checks were obtained from the bank. A total of 83 checks ($40,000) for 2004 through 2006 were embezzled using this scheme.

Regarding the Hertford Supply Company, Ms. Burch had total control over accounts payable like the other affiliate. The illegal transactions followed another process where she created false vendor payments to pay for her personal credit card bills. The checks were issued electronically by Ms. Burch and then, using her position as a manager, she made a request to the IT Department (help desk, Sherry Kiker) saying the payee on a check was made in error and asked that the payee on the accounting record be changed in the accounting software to a vendor who was legitimate.

Again this went undetected until her dismissal because she had total control over the checking account transactions and the bank statement reconciliation. Ann also created expense reimbursements in the name of John Turner, vice president, and cashed them through the company courier to the bank for her own use. Copies of 75 cancelled checks were reviewed, evaluated, and determined to be fraudulent by suspicious endorsements and no supporting documentation. This scheme had taken place for four years. The total fraud from this affiliate was in excess of $140,000.

Dismissal and Prosecution

After her dismissal, Ann called Sherry Kiker (IT help desk) and admitted to the theft of company funds and altered records. Ann Burch asked Sherry not to tell her supervisor of the scheme of changing the payee, thus trying to hide the fraud. The employee did inform management of the conversation with Ann Burch and her scheme to steal from the company. The day after Ms. Burch had left the company, she called Ms. Kiker to see if she spoke with anyone about the fraud and Ms. Kiker said she could not talk with her.

In early January 2007 the critical point occurred when Ann Burch could not produce specific credit card receipts requested by her supervisor, Gail Owens. After repeated requests, Ms. Burch admitted to Ms. Owens she had stolen from the company by issuing fraudulent checks. She also admitted to the chief financial officer that she had misused company credit cards by making purchases for herself. Some of the merchandise she purchased was sold to other people to raise cash for her own personal expenses. Among many personal items she purchased were concert tickets, furnishings for her home, and a new car. Ann Burch was escorted from the company property and several days later, terminated from her position.

The prosecutor brought criminal charges against Ms. Burch several weeks later for embezzlement of more than $250,000 from the J.L. Kirkpatrick Company. She pleaded guilty to four counts of embezzlement, eight counts each of forgery of an instrument and uttering of a forged instrument and one count of embezzlement of more than $100,000.

Ann Burch's defense attorney argued to the judge to consider that she cooperated with the investigators and explained to the company how she was able to embezzle without being caught. If she had not cooperated, her defense lawyer said, it would have taken much more time and expense for the investigators to discover the schemes. She was also the single parent of two children.

The judge did not agree that her actions would be an extraordinary mitigating factor for which he could reduce the sentence. She was sentenced to a minimum of four years in prison and ordered to pay $5,000 in restitution, which was the amount of the insurance deductible the company had to pay. The judge said "she is a thief and you cannot garnish it any other way."

New Mechanisms

As a result of the fraud committed, the company implemented a number of changes in the responsibilities of the accounting manager's position and internal approval procedures. Duties of the company credit cards were segregated so that one person received the monthly statements and recorded the accounting while her supervisor reviewed the receipts, accounting, and approved the statement for payment.

The cashing of company-issued checks, except for petty cash disbursements, was no longer allowed to be done through the daily bank deposit taken by courier to the bank. Further, the petty cash replenishment received from the bank was delivered by the supervisor of the treasurer's department directly to the supervisor of the department who submitted the original petty cash request. Regarding the two affiliate companies, Shelby Exports and Hertford Supply Company, the accounting duties were segregated among two employees and a supervisor so that no one person had absolute control over accounting entries, disbursements, and bank account reconciliations.

The J.L. Kirkpatrick Company also brought in an outside accounting firm to review the internal controls for the value of their input and to show decisive action to the board of directors.

Summary

A lack of internal accounting controls can be horribly damaging to the small business. Even relatively low-level, nondescript employees can take advantage of openings that allow for massive fraud, with significant consequences. Establishment of the proper oversight mechanisms in coordination with your CPA is the best preventative.

(And Finally!) Profound Insight #16

An auditor is having a hard time sleeping and goes to see his doctor.

"Doctor, I just can't get sleep at night."

"Have you tried counting sheep?"

"That's the problem—I make a mistake and then spend all night trying to find it."

Best of the Best

The following individuals have been recognized via nomination by their peers as offering exemplary service and expertise.

Insurance Advisors

Mark Boehm, MBA, CWPP™

Mark Boehm, MBA, CWPP™ offers expert advice on all things life insurance and life settlement related. Co-author and contributing editor (with Lance Wallach) of *How To Protect Your Clients From Fraud*, Mr. Boehm is known as a straight-talking advisor who takes his fiduciary responsibilities seriously. He specializes in advanced planning strategies for businesses (both large and small) and high-net-worth individuals, and both retail and institutional life settlements consultation. Mark offers completely independent, objective, and nonbiased advice.

Mark Boehm | 972.395.8464 | alphawealth@verizon.net | www.thesafereturn.com

Investment Advisors

Ryan Hill

Ryan Hill, managing partner, Nexus Advisors, LLC, provides specialization in 401(k) and pension plans for closely held businesses. Mr. Hill uses a 6-Step Retirement Plan Solution to deliver greater employer and employee satisfaction. The Retirement Plan Solution's true value is demonstrated through optimizing plan design options for owners and highly compensated individuals. In addition to educating retirement plan decision makers about their fiduciary liabilities, Ryan's 6-Step Solution provides full fees transparency to providers as well as participants. Ryan's primary market is the Dallas/Ft. Worth Metroplex in North Texas.

Aaron Skloff, AIF, CFA, MBA

Aaron Skloff, AIF, CFA, MBA, received a Bachelor of Science (BS) degree in accounting from Pennsylvania State University's Smeal College of Business and Master of Business Administration (MBA) degree in finance from New York University's Stern School of Business. He is a Chartered Financial Analyst (CFA), a member of the CFA Institute (formerly the Association for Investment Management and Research), and an Accredited Investment Fiduciary (AIF). Aaron is CEO of Skloff Financial Group, a Register Investment Advisor firm based in Berkeley Heights, New Jersey. The firm specializes in financial planning, investment management, and risk management for individuals and families and group benefit for employers.

Perry L. Smith, CWPP, CAPP, CLU, ChFC, RFC, MS, R

Perry L. Smith attended Gonzaga University and Eastern Washington University receiving his Bachelor's degree in business and finance, and his Master's of Science in Taxation from Golden Gate University. His securities licenses Brokers and Principal are held at Cambridge Investment Research, Inc., and are associated with their Registered Investment Advisor for Asset Advisory Services.

Perry holds a current real estate license with Coldwell Banker Bain, and has earned the advanced professional designations Chartered Life Underwriter (CLU) and Chartered Financial Consultant (CHfC), from the Society of Financial Service Professionals (SFSP) and the (RFC) from the International Association of the Registered Financial Consultants (IARFC). Earned the Certified Wealth Preservation Planner (CWPP) and Certified Asset Protection Planner (CAPP) designations from the Wealth Preservation Institute (WPI). He is a member of the Society of Financial Service Professionals (SFSP), the International Association of Registered Financial Consultants (IARFC), the Financial Planning Association (FPA), and a member of the East King County Estate Planning Council (EKCEPC), a member of the Asset Protection Society (APS) and the Washington State Representative for the Asset Protection Society (www.assetprotectionsociety.org).

Bill Tsotsos

A former CPA and investment advisor, Mr. Tsotsos has been involved with the life settlement industry since April 2003 primarily representing a national life settlement brokerage. He has written a dozen or so articles on the secondary market for life insurance and offers life settlement advisory services along with litigation support services. He has also been featured on a Southern California financial-oriented radio show on the subject of life settlements.

Law

Richard A. Behlmann

Mr. Behlmann is the founder of the Behlmann Law Firm, LP, and has been practicing law for 30 years. Mr. Behlmann's practice covers estate planning, elder law, business counseling, and

209

wealth preservation. His recently published book, *Avoid the Five Biggest Mistakes in Estate Planning,* was written for a general audience to point out common misconceptions and errors in estate planning and asset protection.

He is a member of the Texas Bar, the Missouri Bar, the American Academy of Estate Planning Attorneys, the National Academy of Elder Law Attorneys, the Texas Bar College, and served as a member of the Texas Bar Association Securities Law Committee. Mr. Behlmann was formerly a CPA—Tax Consultant with both Alexander Grant and Touche, Ross & Company.

James L. Moore, JD

James L. Moore, JD, Counselor at Law, principle and founder of the Law Offices of James L. Moore, PC, is known as the "expert's expert." Moore has 30 years of experience as an estate planning, business succession, and tax attorney helping hundreds of clients plan for, protect, and preserve their personal estates and businesses.

As a Senior Contributing Fellow with the National Network of Estate Planning Attorneys and a former member of the National Advisory Council of the U.S. Small Business Administration appointed by then President Ronald Regan, Moore is a sought-after speaker and legal strategist. He has spoken to groups of tax, legal, financial, and other business professionals ranging from small business owner retreats to 5,000 participant weekend personal development seminar.

Business Services

Carl Allen

Mr. Allen is the owner of Allen Financial Services, LLC. He is a graduate of North Carolina State University (BS Mathematics, 1972) and Durham Technical Community College (AAS

Accounting, 1976). Mr. Allen is currently a member of the Association of Certified Fraud Examiners, the National Association of Tax Professionals, and the National Society of Tax Professionals. He is a volunteer representative for the NC State University Student Aid Association, and provides support and resources for Elon University students pursuing opportunities through their career center.

He provides accounting and technical support for small businesses in the areas of: fraud investigations, interim accounting management support, accounting and project consulting, and income tax preparation and planning.

Barbara Ann Artusa, ATP, CWPP

Barbara Ann Artusa, ATP, CWPP, is the owner of TBA Financial & Accounting Services in Valley Stream, New York and Las Vegas, Nevada. Barbara has been in business for 31 years and provides tax, accounting, investment, incorporation start-ups and insurance services. She's a member of Million Dollar Round Table, NATP, NSTP, CWPP, and ACAT.

Joseph J. Bergey

Joseph J. Bergey is a construction estimator/cost engineer specializing in commercial and residential building construction services and consulting. He has collaborated with real estate professionals, general contracting and construction management firms, and various specialty subcontractors on projects of all types, including corporate offices, hotels, high-rise residential, luxurious high-end homes, private retail, municipal/public works and government, healthcare, schools, and institutions. His estimating specialties involve the following competitive bidding, quantity surveys, material takeoffs, and cost consulting in all architectural, civil, and structural disciplines.

www.AEC-Construction-Estimating.com

Amy L. Kaiser

Amy L. Kaiser, founder of Executive Benefit Solutions Inc. (EBS), is a certified public accountant with more than 12 years of consulting experience on issues ranging from nonqualified deferred compensation, employer-owned life insurance, strategic tax planning, audit defense, federal and state taxation, and bank compliance. Amy is currently dedicated to helping companies keep their best people through customized benefit plans and third-party administration. As an independent consulting firm, EBS also serves as a technical advisor and resource for independent BOLI/COLI groups and national consulting firms.

Sandra Simmons

Sandra Simmons of Money Management Solutions Inc, in Clearwater, Florida is a veteran business cash-flow management expert with an outstanding track record in turning around financially struggling companies. Ms. Simmons, a published author, delivers training seminar/workshops across the United States to business owners on cash flow management.

Steve M. Sorey

Steve M. Sorey, Vice President with Employers Direct Health, is an employee benefits and HR/MIS (Human Resource/ Management Information Systems) specialist. His expertise lies in employee and executive benefits plan design, and leveraging down the cost of the human resource function through the implementation of customizable technology solutions.

Epilogue

Hopefully, you found this book useful in pointing out a few of the more common traps set for the unwary client by clever salespeople. We outlined some proposed solutions to a few of the more obvious issues, but we heartily recommend a healthy dose of the fraud preventative—continued education. Toward that end, the authors steer you to the following recommended Web-based sources of information. Read, and enjoy.

Advanced Tax Commentary	www.taxlibrary.us
Client-Centered Advice	www.financeexperts.org
Financial Advice	www.financeExperts.org
Health-Care Cost Reduction	www.vebahealthcare.com
Investment Consumer Information	www.finra.org/
Legal	www.lawyer4audits
Life Insurance Consumer Information	www.pueblo.gsa.gov/acli/
Life Settlements Information	www.thesafereturn.com
Tax Reduction/Welfare Benefit Information	www.vebaplan.com
Tax Rules and Regulations	www.irs.gov

About the Author

Lance Wallach, CLU, CHFC

National Society of Accountants Speaker of the Year

Lance Wallach, member of the AICPA faculty of teaching professionals and an AICPA course developer, is a frequent and popular speaker on retirement plans, financial and estate planning, reducing health insurance costs, and tax-oriented strategies at accounting and financial planning conventions. He speaks at more than 20 meetings per year, including the annual national conventions of the American Association of Attorney—Certified Public Accountants, National Society of Accountants, National Network of Estate Planning Attorneys, National Association of Tax Practitioners, National Association of Enrolled Agents, National Association of Health Underwriters, American Society of Pension Actuaries, Employee Benefits Expo, Health Insurance Underwriters, NAPFA, NAIFA, FPA, NABA, ALPFA, various state CPA societies, Tax Institutes, medical and insurance conventions, CLU Societies, CPA/Law Forums throughout the United States, and Estate Planning seminars.

He has authored numerous books including *The Team Approach to Tax, Financial and Estate Planning, Avoiding Circular 230 Malpractice Traps and Common Abusive Small Business Hot Spots,* and *Sid Kess' Alternatives to Commonly*

Misused Tax Strategies: Ensuring Your Client's Future, all published by the AICPA, and *Wealth Preservation Planning* by the National Society of Accountants. His newest books *CPAs' Guide to Life Insurance* and *CPAs' Guide to Federal and Estate Gift Taxation* were published in spring 2009 by Bisk CPEasy.

Mr. Wallach has written for numerous publications including the *AIPCA Journal of Accountancy, AICPA Planner, Accounting Today, CPA Journal, Enrolled Agents Journal, Financial Planning, Registered Representative, Tax Practitioners Journal, CPA/Law Forum, Employee Benefit News, Health Underwriter, Advisor,* and the *American Medical Association News.* Mr. Wallach is listed in *Who's Who in Finance and Industry* and has been featured on television and radio financial talk shows, including National Public Radio's "All Things Considered" and NBC television.

Plainview, New York (516) 938–5007 / (516) 9357346
lawallach@aol.com, www.vebaplan.com

About the Contributors

Mark Boehm, MBA, CWPP

Mr. Boehm received his Bachelor of Science (BS) degree from Cornell University School of Agriculture and Life Sciences, and Master of Business Administration (MBA) degree from Southern Methodist University.

A Certified Wealth Planning Practitioner, Mark is a principal with Alpha Wealth Management, a boutique financial services firm providing Asset Protection, Tax Reduction, and Advanced Financial Planning strategies for a high-net-worth clientele.

Dallas, Texas (972) 395–8464
alphawealth@verizon.net, www.alphawealth.org

Aaron Skloff, AIF, CFA, MBA

Mr. Skloff received a Bachelor of Science (BS) degree in accounting from Pennsylvania State University's Smeal College of Business and Master of Business Administration (MBA) degree in finance from New York University's Stern School of Business. He is a Chartered Financial Analyst (CFA), a member of the CFA Institute (formerly the Association for Investment Management and Research) and an Accredited Investment Fiduciary (AIF).

He has taught finance courses through Rutgers University. Mr. Skloff's equity research reports have been published on the two largest financial research databases, First Call and Multex. During the course of his professional career, he has been cited by Associated Press, *BusinessWeek, Dow Jones, Fortune, Princeton Business Journal, Reuters, Wall Street Journal* and other news organizations.

Aaron Skloff is CEO of Skloff Financial Group, a Register Investment Advisor firm based in Berkeley Heights, New Jersey. The firm specializes in financial planning, investment management, and risk management for individuals and families and group benefit for employers.

Carl Allen, III

Mr. Allen is the owner of Allen Financial Services, LLC. He is a graduate of North Carolina State University (BS Mathematics, 1972) and Durham Technical Community College (AAS Accounting, 1976). Mr. Allen is currently a member of the Association of Certified Fraud Examiners, the National Association of Tax Professionals, and the National Society of Tax Professionals. He is a volunteer representative for the NC State University Student Aid Association, and provides support and resources for Elon University students pursuing opportunities through their career center.

Mr. Allen has served in various financial management positions over the past 30 years with companies in the insurance and construction industries. He provides accounting and technical support for small businesses in the areas of fraud investigations, interim accounting management support, accounting and project consulting, and income tax preparation and planning.

Index